Where To Go

A Guide to Manhattan's Toilets

Vicki Rovere

Key to Listings

RR	Restroom
MR	Men's Room
WR	Women's Room; Ladies' Room
L	left
R	right
TP	toilet paper
WA	wheelchair accessible
PG	playground
(3-4)	Intersecting streets or avenues. If the address is an AVENUE, numbers in parentheses are STREETS, and vice versa
6 Ave	= Avenue of the Americas
Lex	Lexington Ave.
Mad	Madison Ave.
Col	Columbus Ave.
Amst	Amsterdam Ave.
FDB	Frederick Douglass Blvd.= 8th Ave.
ACP	Adam Clayton Powell, Jr. Blvd. = 7th Ave.
MX	Malcolm X Blvd. = Lenox Ave.
PAS	Park Ave. South
7AS	7th Ave. South
Bwy	Broadway
WSE	Washington Square East
CPW	Central Park West
CPS	Central Park South
EEA	East End Ave.
WEA	West End Ave.
RSD	Riverside Drive
FDR	Franklin D. Roosevelt Drive

❖ *Contents* ❖

A1 H2 X2 D3 U2 P1 K1 V1 R1 E2 R3 L1 G3 S1 E1 D2 S1 E2 V2 G1 F1 D1 D2 R2 V3 G2 C G4 U3 E7 L8 C4 G7 C5 G6 E4 C8 C7 C1 C2 G5 M1 A2 U1 E5 D4 V4 E6 A3 J1 A1 M2 Y1

Wash. Ave? 61. ∅

U3 = New Yohan

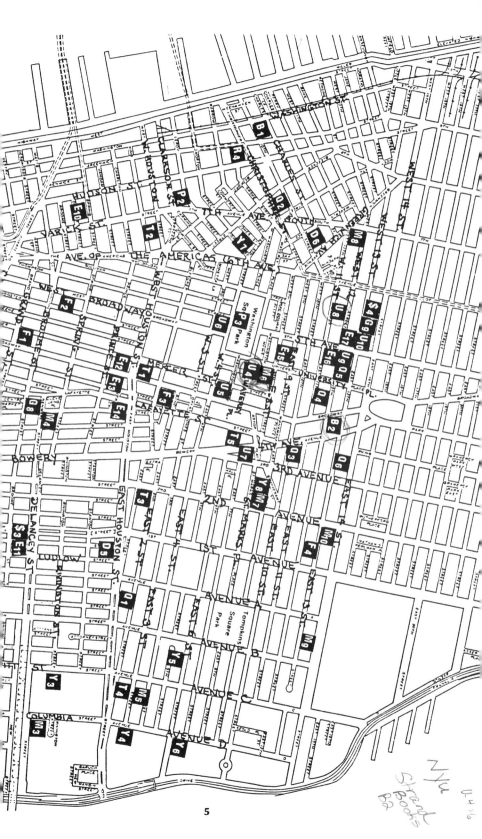

5

NYU
Street
Books
BB

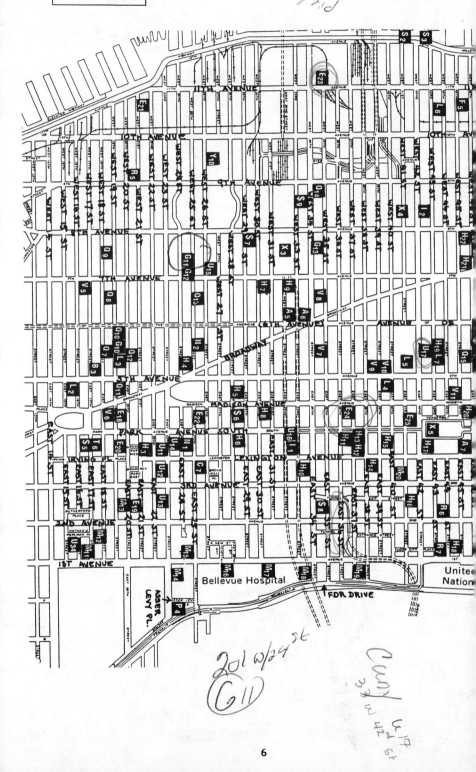

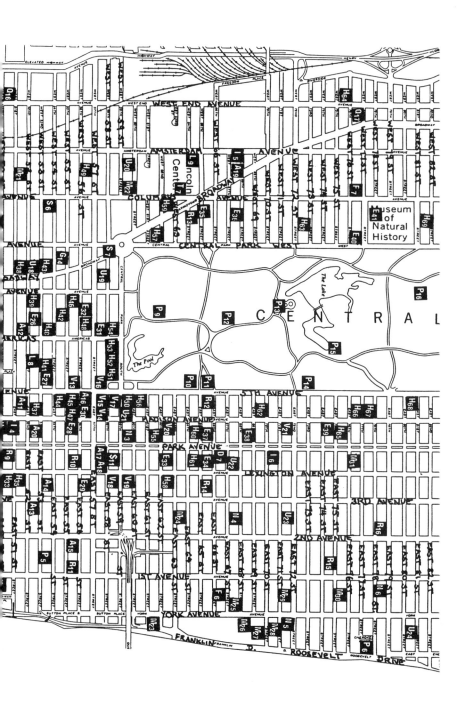

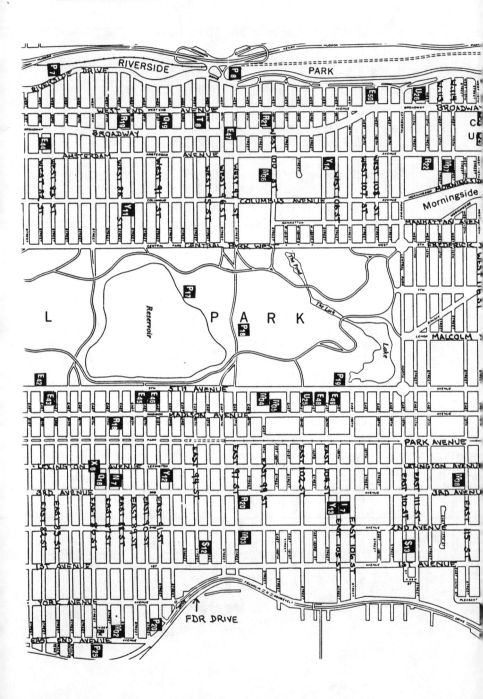

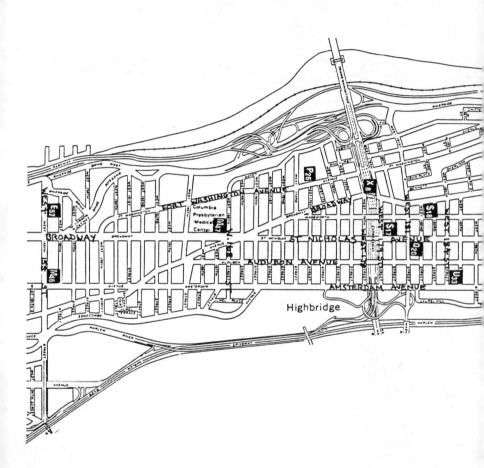

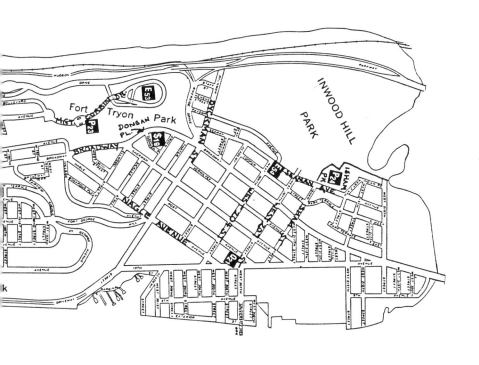

Several years ago, I started walking twelve miles a day for exercise. During the hot summer, I deferred some of my mileage till the evening. One of my routes was up First Avenue, past Stuyvesant Town and the hospitals. Fewer cross streets speeded my progress; it was dark, cool, pleasant.

Somewhere along the way, my bladder would begin to feel full. Could I hold out till 42 St., and head over to Grand Central Station? After 10 or 11 p.m. my options seemed limited. Once in desperation I ventured into the Bellevue Hospital Emergency Room. They graciously allowed me the use of their facilities, which were of a filthiness to equal the public toilets of Autun, in the south of France. Although my leg muscles were not developed for squatting, I squatted.

That time probably inspired the idea for this book. Little did I suspect then that First Avenue was lined with toilet facilities that I could have accessed for the asking!

NOTES ON AMERICAN LANGUAGE USAGE
FOR VISITORS FROM OTHER COUNTRIES

When we are looking for a room in which to eliminate waste products from our bodies, Americans don't say "toilet" much. More often, "toilet" is used to refer to the appliance itself (although you will hear TV commercials mentioning the "the bathroom bowl"). "Bathroom" is quite common, even if no bathtub is in the room. The commonest expression of need is "I have to go to the bathroom," often shortened, especially by young people, to "I have to go." (Hence the title of this book.)

In public spaces, where no bathtub is expected, the facilities are most often called "restrooms" or are divided by gender into "Ladies' Room" and "Men's Room." (Some feminists prefer "Women's Room.") Less commonly you'll find "washroom" or "lavatory." Occasionally you'll see "Powder Room" or "Ladies' Lounge" and perhaps "Men's Lounge" as well. "W.C.", for the English "water closet," is rare here.

In speech, those who prefer euphemisms speak of the "little girl's" or "little boy's room." Less refined are "can," "john," and "head" (from naval usage).

The Blue Ribbon for Persistence in the Face of Adversity goes to a New Jersey friend-of-a-friend, who was traveling into New York on a commuter train.

An urgent need for a restroom struck her. The train had none.

At the next stop she raced off the train and into the station. The Ladies' Room was locked. She dashed back to the train, which hadn't yet left, and rode to the next station. There, she raced off the train, into the waiting room. The Ladies' Room there, too, was locked. She dashed back to the train.

The fourth station had an unlocked restroom.

World Financial Center
West St - Hudson R., Vesey - Liberty Sts.
Open 24 hours
In the Winter Garden, facing semicircular
marble steps: behind/under the steps,
there's a semicircular arcade labeled "Winter
Garden Gallery Shops." The WR is on the R
side, the MR on the L. Leading north off the
Winter Garden is "Courtyard Shops &
Restaurants." More RRs there.

 **Continental Insurance Gallery &
Atrium**
180 Maiden Lane (Front St.)
M - F 10-4
The gallery entrance is behind the escalator.
There's a performing platform on the R side,
tables & chairs on the L. The single-unit RRs
are at back R, to R of the shoeshine stand: 2
doors flush with the wall, with very discreet
brass pictographs. The MR is the first door,
the WR the second. Not WA.

 South St. Seaport
Fulton Market/11 Fulton St. (Front & South)
8 am - 12 pm
RRs on mezzanine on the Front St. side at the
back (Beekman St.). WA. Pier 17 RRs open
10 am - 1or 2 am, on 2nd level.

 East Broadway Mall
East Broadway (Market - Forsyth)
There are RRs at the upstairs restaurant, Triple
Eight Palace. Head back L, R, then L.

 A & S Plaza
6th Ave. (32-33)
*M, Th & F 9:45 - 8:30; Tu & W 9:45 - 6:45; Sa 10 -
6:45; Su 11 - 6*
MR: Concourse 1, 4; WR: Concourse 2, 2, 4,
6. More RRs in Food Court in 7.

 Herald Center
6th Ave. (33-34)
10 - 7 daily
Take express elevator to Food Court on 8th
floor.

 Park Avenue Atrium
237 Park Ave. (45-46)
Entrances also at 111 E. 45 St, 100 E. 46 St.
and 466 Lexington Ave. Varied exhibits:
crafts, cartoons, etc. RRs are in Colors
restaurant.

 575 Fifth Avenue, Retail Atrium
575 5th Ave. (47)
7am - midnight
Entrance also on 47th Street. RRs downstairs.
"This bathroom is locked. Staff at the
Concierge Desk will open on request."
Concierge desk is on main floor at back of
bldg.

 Crystal Pavilion
805 3rd Ave. (49-50)
M - F 8am-10 or 11pm; Sa 9-5
(Entrances also on 3 Ave. and E. 50 St.) Go
downstairs; facing the waterfall, RRs are on
the L.

 Worldwide Plaza
8-9 Aves., 49-50 Sts.
Open 24 hours
The outdoor park part of the Plaza is halfway
between 8th & 9th Aves, & 49th & 50th Sts.
The RRs are in an arcade on the east side of
the park. Get the key from the security guard
inside the bldg. When I visited, the RRs were
closed for repair.

 Olympic Tower
E. 51 St. (5 - Mad); E. 52 St. (5 - Mad)
Daily 7am - midnight
The RRs are just south of the public seating
area, down a short curved corridor.

 Paine Webber
1285 6th Avenue (51-52)
M - F 7am-6pm
RRs on lower level. See a nearby guard for
access. There's an exhibit in the lobby and at
the Equitable Center Atrium in the next
building (787 7th Ave. - hours Tu, W, F 11-5;
Th 11-7:30; Sa noon-5). The concourse
connects to the Time-Life Building (111 W.
50th St.) and the 6th Ave. Subway (47-50 Sts).

 875 3rd Avenue
875 3rd Ave. (52)
M - Sa 7-11; Su & Hol. 11-7
Take the escalator down. See the guard, who
will escort you through mirrored door &
unlock the RR. In the atrium, you'll find a
special bin to donate your soda can to the
homeless.

13

Citicorp Center
3rd - Lex Ave., 53-54 Sts.
RRs open 11 - 8; Bldg closes at midnight

54th St. entrance, closer to 3rd Ave; downstairs.The restaurants are open past 8 pm, and on request will give patrons the key to the staff RRs on the floor below. When I, a non-patron, threw myself on the mercy of a waiter, he fretted about its return, but finally gave over the key, forgoing my offer of my scarf as collateral.

 Manhattan Art & Antiques Center
1050 2nd Ave. (55-56 Sts.)
M - Sa 10:30-6; Su noon-6

MR to R of elevators on 1st & 2nd concourses. WR to L of elevators on 1st concourse.

A16 **Trump Tower**
5th Ave. (56-57)
8 am - 10 pm

Walk to the back of the escalators to descend to the lower level. I hope you're not too suggestible because there's a wall of water cascading at the back. Follow the signs around - L, then R. RRs angle off the same entrance. The signs are so highly polished, they're hard to see: WR - L, MR - R. The paper towel dispensers are almost hidden under the mirrors at the back of the sinks.

 Galleria Atrium
E. 57 St. (Park-Lex)

There are no RRs in the atrium; the guard will direct you to the Palace Restaurant across the street (122 E. 57 St.).

 Place des Antiquaires (The Intl. Ctr. of Art & Antiques)
125 E. 57 St. (Park-Lex)
M - Sa 11-6

There are RRs on both levels, Concourse I & II. Turn R at bottom of escalator; RRs are on the R. If using elevator, turn L, then R. There's a restaurant and a cafe; free lectures are offered once a week or so.

 Cafe Bel Canto
1991 Broadway (67-68)
8 am - midnight; Cafe is open 10 am - midnight.

"This is a public space - users are not required to purchase food or drink." Ask waiter up front for key.

 Park Avenue Plaza
55 E. 52 St. (Mad - Park)
Daily 8am-10pm

(There's an entrance also on E. 53 St.) Just across from the waterfall is a drinking fountain & 2 private unisex toilets.

❖ BOOKSTORES ❖

 Strand
828 Broadway at 12 St.
M - Sa 9:30-9:30; Su 11-9:30

WR on L just past the stairs leading to basement; MR around the corner from there. Check your bags.

 Judith's Room
681 Washington St. (Charles - 10 Sts.)
Tu - Th noon-8; F & Sa noon-9; Su noon-7

("A bookstore for women and their friends.") Check bags at front desk. There's an unmarked RR/storage closet at back on R.

 Barnes & Noble Sale Annex
128 5th Avenue (18)
M - F 9:30-8; Sa 9:30-6:30; Su 11-6

At the back of the store, on the ground floor, is a door with pictographs for Man, Woman & Telephone. There's also a drinking fountain.

 ❖ **COURTS** ❖

 US Court House
40 Centre St. (Foley Square)
M - F 9-5

Go through security check (bag X-ray and walk-through metal detector) & head down the L corridor. "Rest rooms downstairs from exit door."

 NY County Supreme Court
60 Centre St. (Foley Square)
M - F 9-5

RRs are on the 2nd floor. Take the elevator or Stairway C (at the head of the corridor labeled "116, 118 & 119." RR entrances are at the grilled archway overlooking the Centre St. entrance. WR: go up a short flight of stairs, along a corridor & down a short flight of stairs. MR: go up a short flight of stairs... then you're on your own. I also found the sign, "Female handicapped restroom located on 3rd floor." When I visited, the NYS Court Employees Arts & Crafts Exhibit was on in the rotunda.

PEP TALK

They've got us on the defensive: No Public Restrooms.
Restrooms for Customers Only. Don't Even Ask.
   Is it too much to ask? Other countries manage to provide
them. The ratio of public toilets to public telephones here
seems to vary inversely with that of, say, England.
   In this case, when supply diminishes, demand doesn't dry up
in the slightest.
   None of the facilities listed here, with the exception of parks
and playgrounds, are really "public" in the sense that that's their
primary function. Department stores, museums, and train
stations have installed restrooms to serve their customers. If
you're not a customer they will tolerate you, but they're not _for_
you. So these places are really not so different from a
restaurant except that they're bigger and it's therefore not
obvious that you're not a customer.
   As the budget has crunched, social services have collapsed.
Some of this has affected toilet facilities directly (the Parks
Department can't afford to open all its playground facilities) and
some indirectly (addicts can't get off drugs because treatment
programs aren't available, become violent and abusive in
shelters, scare away other residents who then opt to live on
the streets and spend their days in public libraries; one result:
overwhelmed libraries shut their public restrooms). As a
pacifist, I put a lot of the blame on military spending; you may
have your own theory.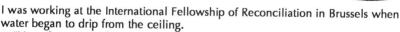
   But surely, if we are going to be part of the life of this city as
tourists or residents we will, from time to time, need to use a
toilet. Now, let's not get snippy with the people who control
our access to these facilities, but let's not let ourselves be
intimidated. When you ask to use the restroom you are making
a reasonable request, and you're offering someone a chance
to exercise his/her humanity in response.
   For months in the research of this book I have asked the
same question countless times: "Hi! Is there a Ladies' Room I
can use?" and the response has been he23eningly positive.

 I was working at the International Fellowship of Reconciliation in Brussels when
water began to drip from the ceiling.
   "How do you say that in English?" asked Charles.
   "It's a leak," I answered. Delighting in my role as language consultant, I also
taught him the expression, "to take a leak."
   Several weeks later, during the Fellowship's Council Meeting in Strasbourg,
Charles, who was the official note-taker, formally excused himself to the
assemblage.
   "I have to take a leak," he explained.

ABOUT RESTAURANTS AND BARS

They're all over town, they're open long hours—some all night. They all have restrooms.

Only most of them seem not to want a visit from you. They post signs to warn you away: "Restrooms for Customers Only." But sometimes they're the only port in a storm. And for some people, they're the option of choice.

First, bars: No one will think it unreasonable if you use the restroom before ordering a drink. So if you're going to get hassled, it'll be on your way out. One friend has suggested tipping the bartender when you ask for the location of the restroom. Of course if the bar is crowded enough you can wander around and find it for yourself, then slip out unnoticed.

Restaurants: I'd suggest looking for a serve-yourself, seat-yourself kind of place with a counter or salad bar. Cafeterias are almost extinct, but fast-food restaurants are the modern equivalent. Pizza parlors are generally friendly. If there's a separate floor for eating, either upstairs or downstairs from the food-service area, there will often be restrooms there. McDonald's Restaurants are all over the place (sometimes open all night) and usually have clearly marked restrooms.

I suspected that the courteous treatment I generally receive has to do with my being a woman, but I've been told of a male cab driver who stops his taxi outside a restaurant and makes a quick visit.

"My cab's double parked," he announces. "May I use the Men's Room?" The employees are usually happy to oblige, and often volunteer to keep an eye on the cab for him.

It's not so hard to understand. Most people have been in a similar situation. If you're polite and neatly dressed, and it's not too much trouble for them, why shouldn't they want to help?

The coffee-shop strategy: If you would feel more comfortable as a customer than you would asking for a favor, order some food to take out. Plastic-wrapped bagels, rolls and pastries are often on display. Save your purchase for later or give it to a hungry person.

Criminal Courts Bldg.
100 Centre St. (White)
Open 24 hours
Walk-through metal detector & hand-held
scanner, no x-ray. Public RRs on 2nd floor,
MR on L, WR on R.

C₄ **NYC Criminal Court**
346 Broadway (Leonard St.)
M - F 9-5
RRs are on the R, about halfway into the
building. (The Clocktower Gallery on the 13th
floor is open W-Su noon-6.)

C₅ **Family Court**
Lafayette St. (Leonard - Franklin Sts.)
M - F 9-5
RRs on ground floor just past security desk
WRs has 2 stalls, one with a door. Walk-
through metal detector & hand check. Very
thorough - they found scissors, pocket knife &
metal fork!

C₆ **Civil Court**
75 Lafayette St. (Franklin - White)
WRs 8 - 5pm, up staircase to R (past mosaic
mural), 2nd floor. MRs 9 - 5pm, up staircase
to L - but closed long term. Warning signs
about safety checks, but none imposed on
me.

C₇ **Appellate Div. of the Supreme Court
of the State of NY**
Lexington Ave. (25-26)
M - F 9-5
Proud of their landmark status, they've
produced a booklet available at the front desk.
Basically, all there is to see is the facade and
the lobby, which are indeed impressive. RRs
are down the L-hand staircase. Women
should ask the guard at the desk for the key
before descending. The WR has a sofa and
coatrack.

❖ RESTAURANTS & BARS ❖ (DINING ESTABLISHMENTS)

D₁ **Fraunces Tavern**
54 Pearl St. (State St.)
M - F 11:30am-9:30pm
The attached museum costs, but you can find
the RRs by turning L before the host's station.

D₂ **Food Court**
70 Broad St. (Beaver)
M - F 6am-7 or 7:30pm; Sa 10-5 or 6
The culinary offerings are Nathan's Famous,
Roy Rogers and Everything Yogurt. RRs are
downstairs. Not WA.

D₃ **Windows on the World**
1 World Trade Center
*M - Sa 7am-10:30am, 3pm-1am;
Su 7am-10:30am, 3 pm-9pm*
At the special elevator in the lobby of 1 WTC,
a uniformed chap will greet you and enforce
the dress code: no jeans, men must wear
jackets and ties. Take the elevator to the
107th floor. For the WR, turn L, and L again in
the midst of the mirrored wall. First you'll
enter a mirrored make-up anteroom. In the
RR, the stalls have tall, louvered doors. The
right-hand stall features a sink with marble
counter and mirror, a vase with fresh flowers
and a linen handtowel. For the MR, (which
reportedly includes a workout room) turn R off
the elevators and go past the host's station
(the Restaurant requires reservations, but the
Hors d'Oeuvrerie doesn't). Both RRs are
attended. When getting off the elevators,
sneak a peak at the view by walking straight
ahead and slightly to the L.

D₄ **St. Margaret's House**
49 Fulton St. (Pearl - Cliff Sts.)
M - F 11:30am-2pm; 4-6pm; Sa, Su & Hols 2-6
The hours given are those of the Cafeteria,
which is open to the public. Prices are lower,
and the atmosphere calmer, than the South
St. Seaport across the way. Look for the
elevators on the R, past the desk. The RRs are
down a short corridor to the L of the elevators.

D₅ **Katz's Delicatessen**
205 E. Houston St. (Ludlow)
Su - Th 7-11; F - Sa 7 - 1am
"Bathrooms are for use of todays [sic]
customers only," so Katz's doesn't really fit
our criteria. But you might enjoy a visit
anyway. Check clippings in the window for
some history. Hang on to the check you're
given at the door (a fast-disappearing deli
tradition) - countermen will punch a price or
write on the back - but even if it's untouched
you'll have to hand it in when you leave. RRs
are at back around the corner to the R.
Takeout options include knishes and hot dogs.
Tourists, how about a can of Dr. Brown's
Cel-Ray to take back home as a souvenir? A
pickle at the back end of the counter will set
you back only 50¢. A couple of vastly-
enlarged letters in the front window convey
thanks to owner Isidore Tarowsky for gift
salamis sent to Presidents Reagan & Carter.
While Mr. T basks in the glow of feeding the
well-fed, hungry people look for handouts on
the corner. Maybe one of them would like
your knish?

D6 Suds Cafe
141 W. 10 St. (Greenwich Ave - Waverly Pl.)
M - F 7am-10pm; Sa & Su 8am-10pm
This laundromat-cafe is a few steps below
street level. Customers can await the cycle's
end in the backyard patio or in the cafe on the
L. There's a unisex RR to the L of the cafe.

D7 Seventh Regiment Armory
643 Park Ave. (66-67)
Tu - Sa 5pm-9pm (Sept.- June)
The hours given are those of the restaurant on
the 4th floor. Go L down a darkened
(atmospheric) hallway to the elevator. RRs are
L of the entrance to the bar.

❖ MUSEUMS, GALLERIES & EXHIBITIONS ❖

E5 Chinatown History Museum
70 Mulberry St. (Bayard St.)
Su - W noon-5
Free admission. Entrance is on Bayard St.
Walk upstairs to 2nd floor. The entrance to
the RR is camouflaged by a giant blown-up
photo at the end of the hall. Go through that
door (if it's locked, ask for key) and you'll find a
single-unit RR at back L. (The Asian American
Bookstore is across the hall from the
museum.)

**E1 Marine Museum of Seamen's Church
Institute**
Whitehall St. (State - Pearl Sts.)
M - Sa noon-6
Look for a big sign, "New York Unearthed," in
back of an interesting glass office tower.
Exhibits are on NY's archeology - you can look
at the staff at work. There are 2 unisex WA
RRs on the lower floor. The video in the
elevator reportedly gives the sensation of
traveling down through layers of debris and,
therefore, time. But it's frequently out of
order.

E2 Federal Hall National Memorial
26 Wall St. (Broad St.)
M - F 9-5
Up a steep flight of wide stone steps (atop
which Washington was inaugurated
President), across the rotunda, to the R &
downstairs. Nice facilities. WA, ramp access
on Pine St. - ring bell.

**E3 Whitney Downtown at Federal
Reserve Plaza**
Nassau St. (John - Maiden Lane)
M - F 11-6
Take the escalator downstairs & ask the
person at the desk for the key. The WR key
sticks a little.

**E4 Manhattan Borough President's Office
Art Gallery**
1 Centre St. (Chambers)
M - F 9-5
Take elevator to 19th floor, The exhibit's in the
lobby of the office. RRs with punch-in
combination locks are down the hall to the L
of the receptionist. Not WA. For more-public
RRs in the same building, take elevators at
back R of the South Entrance to the 3rd floor.
Turn L & L again. "Bags subject to inspection"
at entrance.

E6 Asian American Arts Center
26 Bowery (Bayard - Pell Sts.)
M - F 11-6
Once you're buzzed in, it's one strenuous
flight upstairs. Admission free. There's a
unisex RR with a potted plant on the toilet
tank on the R side of the gallery. Not WA.

E7 Franklin Furnace
112 Franklin St. (W. Bwy - Church)
Tu - F 10-6; Sa noon-6
(This is a gallery, library & performance
space.) Downstairs through doorway on the
R, through a red door ("No Smoking"), R, all
the way back. The RR is through a gold door
on the R. (Shower too, but not for you.)

E8 Artists Space
223 W. Broadway (White - Franklin Sts.)
Tu - Sa 11-6
RRs back L.

E9 Art in General
79 Walker St. (Bwy - Lafayette)
Tu - Sa noon -6
Suggested donation $1. Exhibits on 4th & 6th
floors, plus an audiotape in the elevator and a
window installation on the street. RR on the
6th floor, back L around the corner.

E10 NYC Fire Museum
278 Spring (Hudson - Varick Sts.)
Tu - Sa 10-4
Free admission. RRs are on a landing halfway
up the stairs. The museum has a wonderful
collection of antique firefighting equipment,
but there are also very thorough
words-and-graphics exhibits (including an
explanation of what a standpipe is, and the
derivation of "plug uglies.") In a separate
room, there's an exhibit about women
firefighters.

MUSEUMS AND GALLERIES

Museums run by New York City were free until the early 1970s. They then instituted a pay-what-you-wish, but-you-must-pay-something policy. This is now the policy at a number of private museums as well. You can legally offer a penny, if you dare. I've felt comfortable paying 25¢ at public museums and 50¢ at private ones. Hand the money to the cashier and say, "I'm paying fifty cents," or whatever. Only once did I get even a glimmer of a dirty look!

Private galleries also have restrooms - usually unmarked, so you'll have to ask. Galleries are clustered in Soho and the Upper East Side (especially on 57 St. and Madison Avenue); new ones are springing up in the East Village.

HOMELESSNESS

Some homeless people hold down daytime jobs and live in small shelters run by religious groups. Some homeless people live doubled up with relatives. Although their problems are indeed serious, they don't have any more difficulty than most of us in finding public restrooms to use.

The homeless people with the biggest problem are those who live on the street. With ragged clothes, often large bundles of their possessions, and no access to washing facilities, they're unwelcome in restaurants and bars as well as most of the places listed in this book. You may see them in bus and train stations, and perhaps in hospitals, but that's a very limited selection. I was pleased to discover the availability of restrooms in welfare offices; I hope homeless people are permitted access.

I assume that any soup kitchen that offers people a sit-down meal (rather than handing out sandwiches on the street) also offers toilet facilities. Additionally, there are a number of drop-in centers, some with showers as well.

John Heuss House
42 Beaver St.
(212) 785-0744
Men & women over 18

Antonio Olivero Center for Women
257 W. 30 St.
(212) 947-3211
Women 25 and older

Moravian Church Coffee Pot
152 Lexington Ave. (30 St.)
(212) 683-4231
Men over 50, women over 30

Enter
170 E. 107 St. (3 - Lex Aves.)
(212) 410-706
Youth up to 19

Covenant House
460 W. 41 St. (10 Ave.)
(212) 613-0300
Youth up to 21

The Street Sheet lists "Where to Go for Food and Help" on the Upper West Side. For a copy, call (212) 581-9604.

Lower East Side Tenement Museum
97 Orchard St. (Delancey-Broome)
M - F 11-4; Su 10-4

Suggested donation: $2. There are 2 unmarked toilets in the hall on the L, survivors of the time when toilets were in the hall, not in the apartment. To turn on the light, pull the string at the front, not the chain to the water closet farther back.

 New Museum of Contemporary Art
583 Broadway (Houston - Prince)
W, Th, Su noon-6; F, Sa noon-8

Suggested admission: $3.50. WR: turn L at the 2nd pillar. MR:?

 Alternative Museum
594 Broadway (Houston - Prince)
Tu - Sa 11-6; October - May

The Museum is on the 4th floor (Suite 402) of a building full of galleries. Use the elevator bank on the L. Suggested admission is $3, but they're not pushy about collecting it (or any fraction thereof). Ask for a RR key at the desk and head down the hall, turning R a bunch of times.

 Pratt Manhattan (gallery)
295 Lafayette St. (Houston)
M - Sa 10-5

Take elevator at back to 2nd floor. RRs are to R of reception desk.

 Pen and Brush
16 E. 10 St. (Univ. Pl - 5 Ave.)
Tu - Su 1-4

Ring bell to be admitted to an exhibition by women artists (they hold poetry readings, too). The WR is upstairs at the front, with a wonderful old porcelain sink and a towel dispenser affixed vertically. I guess men can use the unlabeled toilet at the back (also upstairs) with adjacent sink.

Salmagundi Club
47 5th Ave. (11-12 Sts.)
Daily 1-5

The art exhibit starts upstairs, continues downstairs in the poolroom, on the way to which the WR is on the L. The MR is at the R front of the poolroom. At the entrance to the poolroom, just as you leave the bar area, a poem is painted on the wall: "These steps for men are sacrosanct/All female poachers will be spanked/Beyond this point may go no distaff/By adamant request of this staff." (This clearly didn't apply to viewing the exhibit; I don't know if it still applies to evening socializing for club members.)

 Forbes Magazine Galleries
62 5th Ave. (12-13)
Tu - Sa 10-4; Th reserved forTours & Advanced Reservations

RRs are at entrance to the galleries, past the guards' desk, to the L. Toilet seats, at least in the WR, are equipped with hygolet™ santary toilet seats: the seat is encircled with a plastic sleeve that advances at the touch of a button. 900 visitors are allowed daily; so far, it's rare for them to have to turn anyone away.

 Theodore Roosevelt Birthplace
28 E. 20 St. (Bwy - Park)
W - Su 9-5

Admission: $1; free to those under 17 or over 61. RRs are straight ahead at entrance. Exhibits in room on R. (Anti-war scholars may be interested in TR's role in precipitating the Spanish-American War and his later receipt of the Nobel Peace Prize.) If you don't stop the solicitous staff, someone will whisk you upstairs for a tour and commentary of the period rooms.

 Police Academy Museum
235 E. 20 St. (2-3 Aves.)
M - F 9-3

Sign in at downstairs desk and take elevator to 2nd floor. The RRs are R off the elevators, on the way to the museum. Displays include guns, badges, newspaper clippings, photos of Murder Inc., fingerprints, bomb squad, historical uniforms, shackling devices, communications equipment, counterfeit money, bank robbery. Cases in the hall chronicle women's fight to overcome discrimination within the force.

 National Arts Club
15 Gramercy Park (Gram. Pk. W.- Irving Pl.)
Daily 1-5

(Gramercy Park is the continuation of E. 20 St.) Go down the steps & jog R. The WR is straight ahead; the MR to the L of it. The WR has swinging louvered stall doors and hexagonal sink basins.

 Dia Center for the Arts
48 W. 22 St. (10-11 Aves.)
Th - Su noon-6 (closes in summer)

Suggested contribution: $2. Check bags at entrance. Private RRs are on the 3rd floor. When I visited, they were labeled US and THEM, following the theme of the show. The gallery-sitter tallied which one people used.

Met Life
24 E. 24 St (Mad - PAS)
M -Sa 10-6

Ask to visit the Gallery; the guard will give you a sticky patch to wear. Follow signs to Auditorium; once inside, RRs are on the R.

Jacob K. Javits Convention Center
655 W. 34 St., 11th Ave (34-38)
Open 24 hours
Toilets, seating areas & food court on lower level.

 Pierpont Morgan Library
29 E. 36 St. (Mad)
Tu - Sa 10:30-5; Su 1-5
Suggested contribution: $5. Take elevator in the Garden Court to lower level. WA. The hours of the bookshop, at Madison and 37th, are M - F 10-5. They plan to install RRs there, too.

 Whitney Museum of American Art at Philip Morris
42 St. & Park Ave.
M - Sa 7:30am-9:30pm; Su 11-7
Guard at front will accompany you to back with electronic card to open door. (He explained 4 crack smokers at a time tended to take over the space when left unlocked.) Leave the RR door open when you leave - it locks automatically when closed, & causes a headache for the guards.

 Museum of TV and Radio
25 W. 52 St. (5-6 Aves.)
Tu, W, Sa & Su   noon-6; Th till 8; F till 9
Suggested admission: $5. WA RRs downstairs - take stairs or elevator. Another set are on the 2nd floor on the L side of the hallway that intersects with the main one.

 Museum of Modern Art
11 W. 53 St. (5-6 Aves.)
Th 5pm-9pm
Admission usually $7; Th 5-9 "pay what you wish." Pick up the Information/ Plan brochure at the entrance. There are RRs on all 5 floors. In July & August, on F & Sa evenings, Summergarden concerts are held from 6-10pm. Enter on W. 64 St (5-6). The night I visited they opened 20 minutes late - the line stretched to the end of the block. But once the crowd was in, entry was easy. Head straight across the courtyard (wending your way around a couple of statues) to the RRs.

 AT&T Infoquest Center
550 Madison Ave. (56)
Tu 10-9; W-Su 10-6
At entrance you'll be given an Access Card to use on the exhibits. Take elevator to the 4th floor (or bypass the exhibits and get out at the 2nd floor). RRs are right by the elevator. Walk or roll down ramps from exhibit to exhibit, till you reach the 3rd floor. Take stairs or elevator to 2nd floor, where you'll find RRs, electronic games, a store and the exit. Games include Electronic Finger Paint, Scramble Your Face, Make Your Own Music Video, and Robot. (The low point of my visit was hitting the giant News Plus screen on my way down the ramp just when it was reporting the details of a gruesome murder.)

 Colombian Ctr. (Permanent Mission of Colombia to the UN)
140 E. 57 St. (Lex - 3rd Aves.)
M - F 11-5:30
In gallery, 1st unmarked door on L leads to M & WRs. Not WA.

 IBM Gallery of Science & Art
57 & Madison Ave.
Tu - Sa 10-6; Su & M closed
RRs downstairs. WA.

 Steinway Hall
109 W. 57 St. (6-7 Aves.)
M - W, F 9-6; Th 9-9; Sa 9-5; Su noon-5
The exhibit space is on the L. The WR, at front R of the piano showroom, is up 2 red-carpeted steps on L. A tin of potpourri stands open on the marble sink. (The R entrance to the showroom leads directly to the WR.) MR:?

 Carnegie Hall Museum
154 W. 57 St. (6-7 Aves.)
Daily 11-4:30
Admission free. Take stairs or elevator to 2 floor. WR back L, MR back R. WA.

 Museum of American Illustrators
128 E. 63 St. (Park - Lex)
M, W - F 10-5; Tu 10-8
Admission free. The door sticks - pull! There's a unisex RR on the lower level at back (3 steps up). A very polite, unobtrusive guard followed me downstairs asnd back up again as I viewed the exhibit.

 China Institute in America
125 E. 65 St. (Park-Lex)
M - Sa 10-5
Suggested contribution: $2. The Gallery is at R of entrance. RRs are L of entrance, L again and downstairs. Not WA.

 Museum of American Folk Art
Columbus Ave. at 65 St. (Lincoln Sq.)
Daily 9 am - 9 pm
Admission is free. Suggested voluntary donation: $2. RRs are at the end of the display space off to your R.

 Swiss Institute
35 W. 67 St. (CPW - Col)
Th - Tu 2 -7
RRs down hall on R, not WA. There's a shower in the WR, but that might be pushing it.

21

E37 The Center for African Art
54 E. 68 St. (Mad - Park)
Tu - F 10-5; Sa 11-5; Su noon-5

Voluntary contribution $2.50. There's an unlabeled unisex RR in an alcove at the front (past the water cooler). You don't even have to pass the admission desk, although it would be polite to ask. And why not take time to visit the museum? It's a lovely small one in a townhouse; the exhibits are thoughtful and well-mounted - and small enough to get through expeditiously. Additional RRs are or the 2nd floor, near the front.

E38 Americas Society
680 Park Ave. (68)
Tu - Su noon-6

RRs at back R.

E39 Whitney Museum
Madison Ave. at 75th St.
Free Tu 6-8pm

RRs - 2nd floor & lower Gallery (downstairs).

E40 Jewish Museum/NY Historical Society
170 Central Park West (77)
Free Tu 10-5

Coats, umbrellas and large bags must be checked on the lower level. While there, pick up the Guide to the Galleries (also available at the admission desk and in the galleries) which will not only show you the location of galleries (and RRs) but lists the current exhibition in each. RRs are on the 1st, 2nd and 4th floors, toward the south side of the building. The 2nd floor WR has a psychiatrist's couch and a filing cabinet containing toiletries (I'd guess the staff's). Stall doors are well-fitting. Not WA.

E41 Museum of Natural History
Central Park West (77-79)
Su - Th 10-5:45; F & Sa 10-8:45; Closed Thanksgiving & Christmas.

Voluntary contribution. Pick up a floor plan at the information desk at the CPW entrance - there are RRs on all floors except the 4th.

E42 Metropolitan Museum of Art
5th Ave. (82)
F & Sa 9:30-8:45; Su, Tu - Th 9:30-5:15

Suggested admission $6. Pick up floor plan from info desk. RRs on all 3 floors. Check your bags.

E43 Goethe Haus
1014 5th Ave. (82-83)
W, F, Sa noon-5; Tu & Th noon-7

(There's a gallery & a library.) RRs are on the 2nd floor. Turn R at the top of the stairs. Black toilets in the WR! Not WA.

E44 Children's Museum of Manhattan
212 W. 83 St. (Bwy - Amst)
W & Th 3-5

Free during time listed to NYC public school students with ID.

E45 National Academy of Design
1083 5th Ave. (89-90)
Free Tu 5-8

MR & WR - 1st floor before you get to the winding staircase. WR - 2nd floor, turn L getting off elevator or,.turn R coming up stairway.

E46 Cooper-Hewitt Museum
5th Ave. & 91 St.
Free Tu 5-9pm

Turn R at entrance - RRs downstairs.

E47 The Broadway Mall Center/ West Side Arts Coalition
Bwy & 96 St. (in the divider 3strip down Bwy)
W 6-8; Sa & Su 12:30-6

This "revitalized Beaux Arts building on the Mall" was evidently built as a public toilet facility. Now the community has rescued it from disuse and turned it into an art gallery. The RR is at back R. It was out of paper when I visited.

E48 Museum of the City of New York
5th Ave. & 103 St.
W - Sa 10-5; Su 1-5; Tu - organized groups & school tours 10-2

Suggested contribution: $4. RRs are shown on floor plans on R side of kiosk in rotunda: RRs in basement - access by stairway to L of rotunda. Nice shop with books, cards, posters, old-fashioned toys.

E49 El Museo del Barrio
1230 5th Ave at 104 St.
W - Su 11-5

Suggested admission: $2. Ground floor - Bear R a few times to single-unit non-WA RR.

E50 Nicholas Roerich Museum
319 W. 107 St. (WEA - RSD)
Tu - Su 2-5

Ring bell for admittance. Unisex RR to R of stairs.

E51 Hamilton Grange National Memorial
287 Convent Ave. (141-142)
W - Su 9-5

Enter downstairs. RRs are to the L. Not WA.

E52 Hispanic Society of America/Audubon Terrace
613 W. 155 St. (Bwy)
Tu - F 1-4:30; Sa 10-4:30

Free admission. RRs are downstairs: WR to the R, MR to the L of the entrance. But go farther: this small museum houses a delightful collection of Spanish paintings, religious carvings, pottery, decorative tiles, carved wooden furniture, religious and secular textiles.

The Cloisters
Ft. Tryon Pk. (Margaret Corbin Dr.)
Tu - Su 9:30 - 5:15
Suggested admission $6. RRs downstairs, through arch to L of bookshop.

 Dyckman House
4881 Broadway (204)
Tu - Su 11-4
There's a box at the entrance for unspecified contributions. There are no restrooms in the house itself, of Revolutionary War vintage, but outside, under the porch to the L of the stairs, is a unisex 2-stall toilet.

❖ FLEA MARKETS (INDOOR & OUTDOOR) ❖

 SoHo Outdoor Antique Market
465 Broadway at Grand St.
Su 9-5 year-round
There's a chemical toilet at Grand & Mercer.

 SoHo Emporium
375 W. Broadway (Broome - Spring)
M - F noon-8; Sa, Su 11-8
Back right door: "BATHROOMS"

 1 Bond Street Flea Market
1 Bond Street (Bwy - Lafayette)
M - Sa 11-?; Su 10-6
RRs are at the rear, MR, WR and Handicapped - all locked. Ask any of the vendors for the key.

CLOSED

 Sirovich Senior Center Thrift Shop
331 E. 12 St. (1-2 Aves.)
M - F 9-3 (see description)
The public is welcome at the thrift shop on the mezzanine - go up the R staircase. Hours depend on who's running it: M, T & W they open 9 or 9:30 & close at 2:00 with an hour off for lunch 11:45-12:45. Th & F hours are 10-3, with lunch closing 12-1. Prices are rock bottom! MR is also on the mezzanine, at the top of the L-hand stairs. WR is on the 2nd floor, one more flight up, just above the MR.

 Salvation Army Thrift Store
536 W. 46 St. (10-11 Aves.)
M - Sa 9-4:45
This flagship of the Salvation Army chain stands out for its acceptance of credit cards (Visa, MC - $50 minimum) and its open-to-the-public RR. It's on the 3rd floor, labeled "Toilet," just to the R of the stairs as you ascend. There is just a toilet - no sink - so if you're carrying a water bottle, it might come in handy here.

 Antiques, Flea & Farmers Market at P.S. 183
E. 67 St. (York - 1st Ave.)
Sa 6am - 6pm
"Girls" to R of L entrance; "Boys" a little farther R. No pets.

 I.S. 44 Flea Market
Columbus Ave. (76-77)
Sun 11-6
Enter the school building near Columbus & 77th St. RRs are halfway down the hall on the R. There's an attendant in the WR.

 Mart 125
260 W. 125 St. (FDB-ACP)
M & Tu 10-6:30; Th-Sa 10-7:30
The ground-floor shops are stocked with African fabrics, jewelry, gifts, etc. A food court (with some health foods) is on the 2nd floor balcony (stairs at front, stairs and elevator at back). Locked Customers' RRs are at back on upper level; ask at any counter for the key. WA.

❖ GOVERNMENT BUILDINGS ❖

 US Custom House
Below Bowling Green
M - F 9-5
Airport-like security. L entrance - US Bankruptcy Court. Take elevator to 5th or 6th floor. Down corridor marked "Whitehall".

 NYC Housing Authority
5 Park Place (Bwy - Church)
M - F 8:30-4:25
Entrance also on Broadway. Take elevator to 2nd floor. Head towards the desk, then turn R for RRs. Or, if you use the Park Place entrance and go upstairs through the door on L, RRs are R at the top of the stairs. (There's a flight of steps and an escalator, which was operating in a downward mode when I visited.)

G3 **Internal Revenue Service**
50 Murray St. (Church)
8:30 - 5

Go in door marked "Public Only". Tell the guard you'd like to use the RR. He'll direct you to Door C in back of him. Go through that door, the other door right behind it, down a flight of stairs & along a corridor to your L. More than half of your tax dollar collected by IRS goes to pay for war - past, present & future. That's one big reason why there's so little money for public toilets.

G4 **City Hall**
Bwy - Park Row, Murray - Warren
M - F 10-4

WR: 2nd floor. MR: Council chamber (2nd floor) & basement.

G5 **The Louis J. Lefkowitz State Office Building**
80 Centre St. (Worth)
7 am - 6 pm

Enter on Centre St., head straight to the back. WR on R, MR on L. Don't be surprised if you see people of an inappropriate gender turning off at the sign - the toilets are down a corridor containing offices.

G6 **NYC Dept. of Health**
Centre - Lafayette Sts., Leonard - Worth Sts.
8:30 - 5, 5:30, 6..

Entrances on all 4 sides, but Leonard St. entrance is a dead end (Burial offices). Entering on Lafayette St. side, take stairway B on the R, past the public telephones. RRs downstairs.

G7 **Jacob K. Javits Federal Building**
Worth - Duane Sts., Bwy - Lafayette St.
M - F 8-5

Visitors enter on Duane St. (Bwy - Laf). Your bag will be x-rayed. Lots of art on the walls. There are public RRs on floors 2, 3, 7,10 and 12; take elevator to all floors, escalator to 2nd and 3rd. On the 2nd floor, MR is at SW corner, WR at NW corner. (On ground floor, the US Govt. Printing Office Bookstore is open daily 8:30 - 4.)

G8 **NY State Dept. of Public Service**
400 Broome St. (Centre-Mulberry Sts.)
M -F 8-4:30

Go L past the elevators, then R. WA. When they have meetings, they may be open till 8 or 9pm.

G9 **HRA Office of Family Services**
11 W. 13 St. (5-6 Aves.)
M - F 9-5

Turn R past the elevators, and R again. The RRs are WA, but there's one step at the entrance.

G10 **NYS Dept of Labor/20th St. Community Service Center**
52 W. 20 St. (5-6 Aves.)
M - W, F 8-5; Th 8-7

WA private MR & WR at L of the waiting area. Get the key at the desk - it's attached to a substantial piece of wood.

G11 **U.S. Immigration & Naturalization Service**
201 W. 24 St. (7-8 Aves.)
M - F 8:30-4

After you pass through the walk-through metal detector & bag search, take the elevator to the 3rd floor, turn L and follow the signs. Not WA.

G12 **US Veterans Association**
252 7th Ave. (24-25)
M - F 7:45-5:10

Walk through the metal detector and take the elevator to the 7th floor. Go L off the elevator, a little L again, then R. Ask the clerk at the desk for the key to the RRs, which she is facing. Not WA.

G13 **NYS Dept. of Labor**
238 W. 35 St. (7-8 Aves.)
M - F 8-5; Th till 7pm

Up a daunting flight of stairs. Get key from guard, who will direct you down a shorter flight of internal stairs.

G14 **NYS Dept of Labor/Community Service Center**
247 W. 54 St (Bwy - 8 Ave.)
M - F 8:30-5

Go through the R doorway; ask guard for key. Private, WA. M & WRs are on R.

G15 **NYC HPD**
157 E. 125 St. (Lex - 3 Ave.)
M - F 9-5

The desk clerk will give you a key. Go through the locked door to the R, make an immediate R to the basement stairs. The RR is a unisex facility with 2 urinals and 2 stalls. For privacy, I moved the trash can I found propping open the door.

G16 **NYC HPD**
W. 133 St. (Bwy - Old Bwy)
M - F 9-noon, 1-4

 Unmarked private RR to L of window. WA

HOTELS

 Marriott Financial Center Hotel
85 West St. (Albany - Carlisle Sts.)
(It's a couple of blocks south of the World Trade Center.) Bear R through the lobby, past the shoeshine stand, to RRs. Or, for a lower-profile entrance, come in via Washington St. (Albany - Carlisle); go down the hall, through the doors, and you'll find the same RRs on the L. This entrance is open 7am-10pm.

 Vista International Hotel
3 World Trade Center (West & Liberty Sts.)
(There's an entrance through 1 WTC.) Go up the circular staircase. RRs are to the R, on the other side of the Vista Lounge.

 Gramercy Park Hotel
2 Lexington Ave. (Gramercy Pk. N. & 22 St.)
RRs to L of entrance.

 Arlington Hotel
18 W. 25 St. (Bwy - 6th Ave.)
Go straight ahead - the unmarked, right-hand door in the back wall holds a tiny unisex RR. A small sink has ingeniously been tucked in above and to the R of the toilet. 3 cloth hand towels hang from a rack.

 The Carlton
22 E. 29 St. (Mad)
Turn L; the last door on the R leads downstairs.

 Chatwal Inn
429 Park Ave. South (29-30)
The "Wash Room" is the second door on the L down the hall.

 Southgate Tower Hotel
371 7th Ave. (30-31)
Turn R before the gates leading to the elevators; follow the pictographs (including up a short flight of stairs).

 Roger Williams Hotel
28 E. 31 St. (Mad)
Restaurant hrs: M - F 11:30am - 10pm; Sa noon - 10; Su closed
There's an entrance from the lobby into the corner restaurant, the Young Fu Noodle Shop. RRs are on your L.

 Ramada Hotel
7th Ave. (33)
Formerly Hotel Pennsylvania, then NY Penta. Ask at the desk, and you'll be given the code to the combination lock for the downstairs RR. Take the elevator, or the stairs at back where it says "Restaurants." Turn R; WR has attendant. Or take elevator to 6th floor and find the Executive Conference Center. RRs are down the hall on R. On L, there's a WA unisex RR and, a little farther along, a WA drinking fountain.

 Dumont Plaza Hotel
E. 34 St. (Lex - 3 Ave.)
You'll be directed to the adjacent restaurant - go all the way to the back.

 Sheraton Park Avenue
Park Ave. (37)
Park Ave. entrance: L, past the lobby; RRs on the L. 37th St entrance: down corridor; RRs on the R. The WR has tall louvered door, fresh flowers on the makeup counter.

 Shelburne Hotel
303 Lexington Ave. (37-38)
L, then R.

 Doral Park Avenue Hotel
90 Park Avenue (38)
Take elevator down to Lower Lobby. There may be a bit of a wait for the elevator.

 Doral Court Hotel
130 E. 39 St. (Lex)
A door labeled Rest Rooms is just to the L of the desk. The corridor has ramps but the RRs aren't WA.

 Doral Tuscany Hotel
E. 39 St. (Lex - Park)
Go R and then R again. WR has embossed TP, tall louvered doors. To return, follow signs to "Time & Again Restaurant", which will lead you back to the lobby.

 Helmsley Hotel
212 E. 42 St. (2-3 Aves.)
Look diagonally R - you'll see the RR sign. The WR has fresh roses floating in little glass bowls.

 Grand Hyatt Hotel
E. 42 St. (Park - Lex)
Go up escalator or stairs to Lobby. To RRs, either aim L of Trumpets Restaurant entrance or head towards Cheney Jewelers and turn R up ramp. WA. RRs are also on Conference Level and Ballroom Level. To wheelchair-access the lobby, contact Security. They'll bring you up by elevator from the Grand Central concourse.

UN Plaza Hotel
E. 44 St. (1-2 Aves.)
Go R, down the corridor to the elevators. Take one to the 2nd floor. Go L off the elevators; WR on L, MR on R.

 Royalton Hotel
44 W. 44 St. (5-6 Aves.)
RRs are in an alcove along the wall on R, just before the food service counter. The WR is very modern. The floor-to-ceiling stall doors form a mirrored wall behind which one has no way of knowing which one (or who) lurks. But try pushing at random. Reportedly the MR is even more spectacular. Not WA.

 The Roosevelt Hotel
E. 45 St. (Mad - Vanderbilt Aves.)
Up stairs, turn R (up some more steps). Not WA.

 Marriott Marquis Hotel
1535 Broadway (45-46)
Enter on B'way or W. 45 St. WA RRs are on levels 3-9, accessible by escalator and elevator. RRs on floors 6 & 7 are on the south side of the building. RRs on floors 3, 4, 5, 8 & 9 are on the north side. If you go up to 9, you'll enjoy the view.

 Milford Plaza Hotel
8th Ave. (45-46)
The RRs are on the ground floor, at back L, across from the entrance to the "Stage Door Canteen" and near the 46th St. entrance. Not WA.

 Paramount Hotel
235 W. 46 St. (Bwy - 8 Ave.)
RRs are on either side of the pay phones at back. The WR has 2 entirely private cabins. They're roomy, but not WA. The TP dispenser holds a rose. To work the faucet, pull the tube outward. Sink basins are etched silver cones signed by the artisan (P. Saballi).

 Roger Smith Hotel
501 Lexington Ave. (47)
The WR is at the top of the stairs to the L of the desk. Elegant! It has geometric designs in black, gray & white marble. Brass fittings; tall stall doors. Not WA. MR: continue around the corner to the L.

 Embassy Suites Hotel
1568 Broadway (47)
Take the elevator to the Main Lobby on the 3rd floor. The RRs are at back L - they're WA except for lack of grab bars.

 Hotel Edison
228 W. 47 St. (Bwy - 8 Ave.)
Entrance also on W. 46 St. Go past the check-in desk and turn L. But you have to ask, because someone will monitor your progress and buzz you in as you reach the door. WA.

 Hotel Inter-Continental
111 E. 48 St. (Lex - Park)
WR: Go straight ahead almost to the back counter, then turn R. WA, but there are 2 steps at entrance. MR: ?

 Marriott East Side Hotel
525 Lexington Ave. (48-49)
Turn R and go upstairs. Turn R and go up the steps or continue down corridor till you reach the "Morgan D" conference room on the L, and go R up the steps there.

 Holiday Inn Crowne Plaza
Broadway (48-49)
Take the escalator up to the lobby. Walk to the back of the escalators and turn L. RRs are WA. When I emerged from my stall, a woman in a black cocktail dress asked me to zip her up. Assuming she had changed from her office clothes and was out for a night on the town, I wished her a lovely evening. On my way out I spotted her photo posted as one of the evening's entertainers.

 Beekman Towers Hotel
5 Mitchell Place (= 49 St. E. of 1 Ave.)
The attached restaurant at this orange-y brick Art Deco building is the Zephyr Grill. The RRs are downstairs; pull the L side of the gate toward you - it's magnetic.

 Doral Inn
541 Lexington Ave. (49-50)
Inside Gallery Bar, make a R, downstairs.

 Waldorf Astoria Hotel
Park Ave. (49-50)
There's also an entrance on Lex. Ave. (49-50 Sts). From the Lex side, take escalator up to lobby. From Park side, take stairs. Coming from Park, the MR is on the L, WR on the R. Definitely not WA: there are several steps up from the lounge to the toilet area. They're all separate rooms, complete with sink. An attendent waits.

 Hotel Beverly
125 E. 50 St. (Lex)
L up the stairs before the restaurant.

 Helmsley Palace
455 Madison Ave. (50-51)
Enter through the courtyard. RRs are upstairs to the L. From the 50th & 51st St. entrances: go upstairs, R, up more stairs. In the WR, fresh flowers are on the makeup counter and at sinks.

 Loew's Summit
51 St. & Lexington Ave.
RRs on the mezzanine. Walk straight through the lobby - stairs to the mezzanine are on the L, across from the elevators. At the top of the stairs, turn L.

26

Omni Berkshire Pl.
E. 52 St. (Mad - 5 Aves.)
Entrance on 52nd St., L halfway into Lobby
seating area.

 Novotel Hotel
226 W. 52 St. (Bwy - 8 Ave.)
Take elevator up to Lobby. Go pretty much
straight ahead - there's a "Restrooms" sign on
a square mirrored pillar. Then another sign will
point you R.

 The Sheraton Centre
811 7th Ave. (52-53 Sts.)
Temporary entrance on 53 St. (6-7 Aves.) Up
ramp to L.

 NY Hilton
1335 6th Ave. (53-54)
Take escalator or elevator to the 2nd floor
Meeting Rooms; RRs are near the back on the
54th St. side. WA.

 Hotel Dorset
30 W. 54 St (5-6 Aves.)
To the back, then L. RRs not WA.

 Rihga Royal Hotel
151 W. 54 St. (6-7 Aves)
Go R, into Halcyon (restaurant). Go past the
singer at the piano and head for the wine rack
- there are stacks of bottoms of wine bottles
facing you, to about 6 ft. high. The RRs are
behind it.

 Ameritania Hotel
Broadway & 54 St.
Two narrow, unmarked doors on either side
of a large potted plant. Cramped but stylish.
Not WA.

 St. Regis Hotel
2 E. 55 St. (5 Ave.)
Downstairs on L, R, down some more stairs,
R to the end of the hall, L. The doors have
brass men's & women's heads on them.
There's an attendant in the WR, and some
perfume spritzers on the sink. Not WA.

 The Peninsula
700 5 Ave. (55)
Straight back (which because of the
architecture, means up & around). Which
unmarked doorway to go through? No matter,
they both lead to the same little foyer, off
which are both the RRs. Not WA.

 Omni Park Central
870 7th Ave. (55-56)
(There's another entrance on 56 St. (7-Bwy).)
The way to the RRs is clearly marked: L, then
R. There's a ramp, and a stall with railings, but
the stall is no larger than the others. The WR
has tall stall doors and a teeny flower
arrangement on each of the sinks.

 The Drake Hotel
E. 56 St. (Park - Mad)
Turn R at the desk, go past the elevators,
down the stairs and follow the signs. There's a
shoe-buffing machine outside the RRs. Lost
when you come out? Follow the signs to the
Lobby Bar.

 Parker Meridien Hotel
118 W. 57 St. (6-7 Aves.)
There's also an entrance on 56th St. RRs are
down the stairs to L of Maurice restaurant. The
MR is at the foot of the stairs, the WR to the R
of it. There's a pay phone in the space
in-between, so that anyone using it will have
to smush him- or herself up against it to let
women visitors through.

 Days Inn
440 W. 57 St. (9-10 Aves.)
Go up a short flight of stairs and head toward
the back.

 Regency Hotel
540 Park Ave. (60-61)
Bear R, go down the hall towards the back.

 Hotel Pierre
2 E. 61 St. (5 - Mad Aves.)
Starting at the desk, make 2 rights, go up two
wooden steps; the entrance is under the
balcony on the R. The WR is on the L; the MR
is on the R. (From the 5th Ave. entrance, the
wooden steps are on the L.)

 Mayflower Hotel
Central Park West (61)
WR: Turn R, make the first L; it's on the R.
MR:?

 Barbizon Hotel
140 E. 63 St. (Lex)
The stairway to the mezzanine is accessible
from both the lobby (E. 63 St.) and the Cafe
(Lex. Ave.). Turn R at the top of the stairs.

 Empire Hotel
W. 63 St. (Bwy - Col)
Go up the stairs and turn L. WR is on the R,
MR on the L, right by the end of the balcony.
The decor in the WR, as in the hotel, is
charming, but the waste baskets were
overflowing. Let's hope when renovation is
complete such glitches will have been ironed
out.

 Hotel Plaza Athenee
E. 64 St. (Mad - Park)
Immediate L, walk to end of corridor, turn R.
There are individually-rolled cloth hand towels
in the WR!

 Mayfair Regent Hotel
E. 65 St. (Park - Lex)

Sharp R at foot of entrance stairs (entrance to Le Cirque).

 The Westbury
E. 69 St. (Mad)

If you use the 69th St. entrance, continue past the desk, through the farthest doorway ("Fire Command Station"). If you enter through "The Polo" on Madison (69-70) jog R, L (through the Exit), then R to end up in the same place.

 Olcott Hotel
27 W. 72 St. (CPW - Col)

Get the key at the desk. The WR is the last turnoff on the L, with a sign "Hotel Guests Only." MR: ?

 Hotel Esplanade
305 West End Ave. (75-76)

The doorway (with the "Max" canopy) to the R of the main entrance will lead you, under an indoor canopy, to the back of the lobby where you will spot pictographs. Open the door, go downstairs & turn R.

 Surrey Hotel
20 E. 76 St. (Mad - Park Aves.)

They'll send you to the Pleiades Restaurant next door. RRs are to the R, past the bar.

 Hotel Carlyle
Madison Ave. (76-77)

Bear L, down a few steps to the foyer. The RRs are through a doorway diagonally L of you.

 The Mark
25 E. 77 (Mad - 5 Ave.)

Go up the circular stairway you'll find before you reach the restaurant. Standing at the top of the steps, you'll see a RR sign diagonally L of you. Go down that corridor & turn L. The stall doors are full-size wooden ones, giving you a European standard of privacy.

 Stanhope
995 5th Ave. (80-81)

RRs in alcove directly to the R of the desk. WR has trompe l'oeil fabric wall covering & spongy paper hand towels (remember Kleenex Dinner Napkins?)

 Excelsior Hotel
45 W. 81 St. (CPW - Col)

This small hotel sends you to the attached coffee shop; there's an unmarked RR in back, on L.

❖ INSTITUTES, SOCIETIES & CENTERS ❖

200 Lex
200 Lexington Ave. (32-33)
M - F 9-4

Walk to back of this designers' building, L, past the elevators into the Designer Lounge. The entrance to the RRs is up 2 steps to the L of the food counter. Not WA.

 Martin Luther King, Jr. Labor Center
310 W. 43 St. (8-9 Aves.)
M - F 10-8

There are periodic art exhibitions, intense and entertaining, in the gallery at R. Even if one's not on, the RR sign and arrow is easily visible L of the guard's desk.

 Japan Society
333 E. 47 St. (1-2 Aves.)
M - F 9:30-8 or 8:30; Sa & Su 11-5

(During the week, open evenings when classes are in session. Otherwise they close at 5pm.) The Gallery is open Tu - Su 11-5. RRs are downstairs on L- MR at front, WR at back.

 The Urban Center
457 Madison Ave. (50-51)
M - F 8am-9pm; Sa & Su 8-6

Enter on the L side of the courtyard of the Helmsley Palace. There's a bookstore and an exhibit on "Architecture and its Allied Arts." The bookstore carries "The Toilets of New York" by Ken Eichenbaum (Litterati Books, $8.95). RRs: go upstairs and turn L.

 Elaine Kaufman Cultural Center
129 W. 67 St. (Bway-Amst)
Su - Th noon-6

Go up the stairway (there's an elevator, too) to the L of the security desk. The MR faces you; the WR is around the corner: go R, then L. WA. The Gallery is to the L off the corridor at the top of the stairs. A plus: live music wafting through the halls.

Asia Society
725 Park Ave. (71)
M - F 10-6:30; Sa 11-6; Su noon-5
The above are the Bookstore hours; the
Galleries, with a $2 admission charge, are
open Tu-Sa 11-6, Su noon-5. RRs: go
downstairs to R of Bookstore. (The Bookstore
definition of Asia seems to include New
Zealand & Papua-New Guinea.)

 Legal Aid Society
230 E. 106 St. (2-3 Aves.)
M - F 9-6
RRs to the R of entrance.

 ❖ JEWELRY EXCHANGES ❖

 Paramount Diamond Exchange
155 Canal St. (Bowery)
M - Sa 9:15-5
(Entrances also on Bowery.) Locked RRs are
downstairs - staircase is at back L. Ask any
salesperson for a key.

J₂ **NY Jewelers Exchange**
70 - 74 Bowery (Canal - Hester Sts.)
M - Sa 9-5:30 (After Thanksgiving, open Su, too.)
Locked RRs are to the R on the 2nd floor (lots
of stairs!). There's a coffee shop on the L.

J₃ **National Jewelers Exchange**
4-8 W. 47 St. (5-6 Aves.)
M - F 9-6
The Diamond Dairy Kosher Luncheonette is
on the mezzanine. Go up the stairs at back R;
the single-unit RRs ("for customers only") are
at the top.

J₄ **The NY Jewelry Center**
10 W. 47 St. (5-6 Aves.)
Locked RRs are downstairs. Stairs are at back
of store; turn L when you reach the bottom.

 Diamond Center of America
36 W. 47 St. (5-6 Aves.)
M - Sa 9-5
RRs upstairs L, locked.

J₆ **World's Largest Jewelry Exchange**
55 W. 47 St. (5-6 Aves.)
M - Sa 9:30-5
RRs are downstairs. Take stairs at back, then
go all the way across the floor. The WR was
locked; the MR door was left open a little.

J₇ **Futurama Diamond Center**
66 W. 47 St. (5-6 Aves.)
M - Sa 9-5
RRs are downstairs at back L; they're locked.
As you walk around, counter people
(especially at the front) will ask "Can I help
you?" There's your opening - ask for the key.

 ❖ LIBRARIES ❖

 SEC Library
75 Park Place (entrance on Greenwich St.)
M - F 9-4:30
Take elevator to the 14th floor, go L down the
corridor. (Follow signs for Public Telephones.)

 The Foundation Center Library
79 5th Ave. (15-16)
M - F 10-5
Take elevator to 8th floor. Turn R & follow the
pictographs. WA.

 **Library for the Blind & Physically
Handicapped**
40 W. 20 St. (5-6 Aves.)
M - F 1-5
RRs - go L past charge desk.

L₄ **Mid-Manhattan Library**
455 5th Ave. (39-40)
M & W 9-9; Tu & Th 11-7; F & Sa 10-6
RR across from, and to L of, stairway. 2 - 5
floors. WA.

L₅ **New York Public Library**
5th Ave. (40-42)
Tu - W 11-7:30; Th-Sa 10-6
WR - inside 42 St. entrance, ground floor &
3rd floor; MR - 3rd floor.

L₆ **NY Public Library - Patents &
Newspapers**
521 W. 43 St. (10-11 Aves.)
Tu - Sa 9-5
Turn L by the guard's desk; once inside the
Reading Room, make a sharp R. The doors of
both W & M are open (for your safety?) but
your privacy is still assured. The cleaning
agent is sweet but unfamiliar: what is that
smell? Be prepared to let the guard inspect
your bags on the way out.

 Mechanics Institute Library
20 W. 44 St. (5-6 Aves.)
*(Sept- Mar) M - Th 9-7 ; F 9-5 (Apr-Aug) open
M - Th 9-6, F 9-5. Closed in July.*

Before the Library entrance, there's a MR on L. Once inside, the MR is to the R, the WR to the L of the entrance. Stop to admire the locking umbrella rack on the R. Also check out the Small Press Center just past it: books are not for sale, but can be ordered from here.

 NY Public Library - Donnell Branch
20 W. 53 St. (5-6 Aves.)
M & W noon-6; Tu & Th 9:30-8; Sa 10-5:30; Su 1-5

The RRs are straight back & downstairs. A WR sign says "NO Hair combing over basin/Undressing/Eating/Bathing." A sign in the front window says, "This table is reserved for chess players on Monday through Thursday from 2 to 5 P.M." And a sign by the return desk says: "With your nose in our books/You may not see the crooks,/Whose records of purse-snatching mount./If you're robbed by these thieves,/While the library grieves/It cannot be held to account."

 Lincoln Center Library
111 Amsterdam Ave. (65)
W - Th 12-8; F - Sa 10-6

Stop at the information desk & pick up "A Guide to The New York Public Library for the Performing Arts." It has floor plans showing the location of the RRs on the Amsterdam Ave. level, the 2nd floor & 3rd floor.

NY Public Library - Schomburg Collection
515 Malcolm X Blvd. (135)
Tu & W noon-8; F & Sa 10-6

Sign in at the guard's desk, then head toward the Auditorium & Shop. Spiffy MR & WR are on your R. Other RRs are downstairs in the Research Library.

HOSPITALS, MEDICAL CENTERS ❖ & SOCIAL WORK AGENCIES

 The NY Infirmary/Beekman Downtown Hospital
170 William St. (Beekman St.)
Daily 8 am - 8:30 pm

Turn R to gift ship, R again down corridor. (The Emergency entrance is on Gold St.)

Gouverneur Hospital
227 Madison St. (Jefferson - Clinton)
Daily 8am - 9pm

Unisex toilet in Walk-In Clinic. R at the entrance, keep going as far as you can, 2 L's past the desk.

NYC Child Health Station/ Baruch Houses
280 Delancey St. (Columbia St.)
The "Patient Restroom," behind & to the L of the receptionist, has an adult-size toilet in a stall, and a child-size toilet in the open.

 Judson Health Center (Gouverneur Hospital)
34 Spring St. (Mott - Mulberry)
See below

M, Tu, Th, F 8:45 - 11:45am, 12:45 - 4pm; W 8:45 - 11:45am, 12:45 - 7pm. RRs on R.

NENA Medical Center
279 E. 3rd St. (Aves. C - D)
M, Tu, Th, F 8:30-4:30; W 8:30-7:30
Private MR & WR are past the guard, on the R.

NYU Health Center
13 University Place (8 - Waverly Pl.)
M - Th 8:30-8; F 8:30-5
L of desk, go down corridor to back. MR is straight ahead, WR on L. The WR has a urinal.

Stuyvesant Polyclinic
137 2nd Ave. (St. Marks - 9 St.)
M - Th 8:30-8; F 8:30-7
There are two doorways in the back wall of the waiting room. Go through the R one all the way down the corridor.

St. Vincent's Hospital
7th Ave South, E. 11 St. & Greenwich Ave.
Open 24 hours
RRs are down the hall to the R alongside the waiting room area. In Emergency, 7th Ave. South (11-12 Sts.), the WR is down the hall to L; I walked in on a woman taking a sponge bath in the sink. MR: ? In the Smith/Raskob Pavilion, 170 W. 12 St. (6-7AS) RRs are to L of entrance. Hours are 7am-9pm daily. Gift shop hours are M - F 9-8, Sa & Su noon-5. Detoured by construction through the nurses' residence entrance, I noticed an ever-so-slightly ominous sign over the mailboxes: "Doctors please close your mailbox after removing mail." Do surgeons need reminders to close up the their patients, too?

 In Gujarat, Gandhi's home state, our tour visited an environmental center concerned exclusively with the design of toilet facilities and their introduction into the community. Our guide showed us one bowl design that required only 3 liters of water to flush and another that required only 1 1/2 liters.

The bowl and surrounding platform would be installed at ground level, and then a circular screen of woven twigs or grasses would be erected around it.

"This has changed the lives of the women," the guide told us. "Before, they would wait until sundown for privacy, and bladder infections were very common. Now they can use the privy in the daytime."

MEDICAL

Even though a hospital entrance may be open 'round the clock, restrooms may not be available outside of visiting hours. Some are; some aren't. Late at night, Emergency Rooms are your best bet.

WOMEN'S GYMNASTICS

This may come as a shock to men who have been criticized for leaving the toilet seat up, but one problem in women's restrooms is that some women should lift the seat but don't.

All of us were taught as little girls about the dangers of "catching things" from public toilet seats. Some of us wipe the seat off first, some line it with toilet paper, some use the tissue-paper seat protectors occasionally found in dispensers. A strategy of some women is not to sit, but to squat over the toilet. It's sort of hard to accomplish this without peeing on the seat. Although it would make sense to raise the seat before attempting this maneuver, it doesn't seem to be a common practice.

Remember those toilet seats in long distance trains that had a spring forcing the seat upright? The only way to keep the seat horizontal was to sit on it. That would solve the problem! Barring the reintroduction of the spring, however, our only defense might be to leave the seat up when we're finished, and hope the practice spreads.

You might also like to know about a gadget marketed to women hikers — something like a plastic funnel, with the spout set at an angle: Sani-fem, P.O. Box 666, Downey, CA. 90241.

Roberto Clemente Family Guidance Center
540 E. 13 St. (Aves. A-B)
M & Th 9-8; Tu, W & F 9-5
The Spanish for "bathroom" is "baño" - it might come in handy here. Public RRs are down the hall on the R, past the staff RRs. Not WA.

 New York Eye & Ear Infirmary
E. 14 St. & 2nd Ave.
From 14th St. entrance: WR - turn R past info desk; MR - go straight through doorway (towards snack cart), turn R. Outpatient entrance around the corner on 2 Ave. will get you to the same place.

 Beth Israel Hospital
E. 16 St. & 1st Ave.
Visiting hours 11-8.
To the L of the entrance.

 Hospital for Joint Diseases/Samuel H. Golding Building
301 E. 17 St. (1-2 Aves.)
Open 24 hours
M & W to the R, past the elevators.

 Cabrini Medical Center
227 E. 19 St. (2-3 Aves.)
Open 24 hours
Turn R at the desk, down the hall, up a mini-flight of steps - WR left, MR right. (Emergency Rm. on 20 St.)

 VA Medical Center
E. 23rd St. (1 Ave. - Asser Levy Pl.)
Open 24 hours
Walk through the metal detector & turn L.

 David B. Kriser Dental Center, NYU
345 E. 24 St. (1-2 Aves.)
Summer hrs: M - F 9-5, weekends closed
During school term, the library's open till 11 at night, & usually there's a guard on duty 'round the clock. Turn L, toward Auditorium, then R.

 Bellevue Hospital
1st Ave. (27)
R inside the doorway is a MR ("closed 7pm - 7am"). Continue down the corridor. Just as you get to the waiting area, past the mini-police station with a bank of TV surveillance screens, a WR is on the L. At the far end of the waiting area, just before Visitor Passes, WR & MR on the L. There's a nice park south of the hospital.

 Schwartz Health Care Center
530 1st Ave. (30-31)
WR is at the end of the long corridor, on the R; MR is around the corner. "To Gain Entry Between The Hours Of 12AM - 6:00PM Please Push Button On Your Left."

 NYU Tisch Hospital/ Rusk Institute
E. 34 St. (1 Ave.- FDR)
Open 24 hours
Go down corridor to L of guard's desk - RRs are on L.

 Bide-A-Wee Home Association
E. 38 St. (1 Ave.- FDR)
M - Sa 8:30 -7; Su 10-6
The RRs are at R front.

 Blue Cross/Blue Shield Customer Service Center
622 3rd Ave. (40)
M - F 8:30-5
Walk downstairs. You'll be in a stairwell surrounded by 3 unmarked doors. Open the door on your L (or take the elevator) and follow the RR signs around through several twists & turns.

 St. Clare's Hospital & Health Center
426 W. 52 St. (9-10 Aves.)
Open 24 hours
Emergency: Turn R, go down hall. RRs are on L. WR is before MR, but you'll have to make a sharp L to see it. The entrance at 415 W. 51 (9-10) is open 7am-midnight. Go straight down hall from guard's desk; turn R.

 St. Luke's - Roosevelt Hospital Center
428 W. 59 St. (Col-10 Ave.)
You must stop at the guard's desk at both the above & following locations. Go up steps behind guard, turn R to a unisex RR. Columbus Ave. (58-59): Go up steps, past guard; the RRs are down the hall on the R past the fire extinguisher.

 The Animal Medical Center
510 E. 62 St. (FDR Drive)
Open 24 hours, but you have to ring for the attendant after 11pm.
Go up the ramp; at the top, the MR will be facing you. For the WR, make 2 L's and yet another along the corridor you'll find yourself in.

 Manhattan Eye, Ear & Throat Hospital
210 E. 64 St. (2-3 Aves.)
24 hours
Turn R to RRs.

 Memorial Hospital
1275 York (67-68)
24 Hours
Go past the escalators; RRs are a short way down the corridor, on the L.

 NY Hospital: Lying-in Hospital/Woman's Clinic
525 E. 68 St. (York - FDR)
6 am - 8 pm
Also accessible from 70 St. There's a WR to the R of the entrance. MR? (Emergency: just west of the Lying-in Hospital on 70 St.,)

HAVE YOU TRIED...?

Political campaign storefronts
Funeral parlors
Gas stations
Storefront medical clinics/doctors' and dentists' offices/group practices
HIP centers
Animal hospitals
Christian Science Reading Rooms
Health clubs/weight-loss clinics
Portable toilets left unlocked at construction sites
Martial arts studios
Churches
   during bazaars
   evenings when AA, etc. meetings are scheduled
   anytime
Parking garages
Labor union HQs
Community service groups in poor neighborhoods
Police stations
   If these are the people who'll arrest you for peeing in the street, aren't they
   morally bound to offer you an alternative?
Housing project community centers
Firehouses
Nursing homes
Senior centers
Auto showrooms
Theaters at intermission
   Supposedly there's a tradition of penniless drama students mingling with the
   sidewalk crowd at intermission and then sneaking in to see the second half of
   the play. If you time it right you can use this ploy to get on the restroom line.
   (Likewise, you may be able to enter a movie theater for free after the last
   showing has started.)

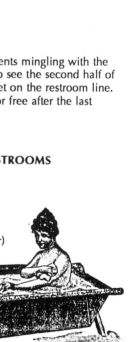

PLACES YOU'D THINK WOULD HAVE PUBLIC RESTROOMS BUT DON'T

Empire State Building
St. Patrick's Cathedral
The Woolworth Building
Tower Records
Unification Church HQ (at Hotel New Yorker)

New York Hospital
525 E. 68 St.; 520 E. 70 St.
The Main Entrance is on 68th St. Walk straight down the corridor past the Gift Shop, then turn L.

The Hospital for Special Surgery
535 E. 70 St. (York- FDR)
The main entrance is off a driveway cutting between 70 & 71 Sts., on the R. The RRs are L of the information desk.

Strang Cancer Prevention Center
428 E. 72 St. (York - 1 Ave.)
M - F approx. 8-5
Take elevator to LL; turn R. The unmarked door at the end is a large, private RR. Not WA.

Gracie Square Hospital
420 E. 76 St. (1st - York Aves.)
Daily, maybe 8 - midnight
Turn L; there are 2 doors with "Lavatory" signs flanking a corner.

Lenox Hill Hospital
100 E. 77 St. (Park - Lex)
Open 24 hours
RRs are on the L. Emergency is at 120 E. 77 St. The Clinic, open 7:15-5pm, is at 110 E. 77 St.

Beth Israel Hospital North
East End Ave. (87-88)
(Formerly Doctors' Hospital.) The guard points me down the L corridor: "Second door on your L." It's unmarked but turns out to contain the right equipment. Men, you'll have to do your own asking! (The EEA entrance closes at 10pm but Emergency on 88th is always open.)

Metropolitan Hospital Center
E. 97 St. & 2nd Ave.
The main entrance is in back of the parking lot on E. 97 St. (1-2). Not knowing this, I entered through the Psychiatric Pavilion on 2nd Ave. and was directed around many corners until I reached Information. RRs are just off the lobby.

Mount Sinai Medical Center / Klingenstein Pavilion
5th Ave. (99)
Open 24 hours
Turn R at guard's desk.

Mt. Sinai Hospital
Madison Ave. & 100 St.
Open 24 hours
New bldg. - smoke free pavilion. Up steps, sharp R.

Riverside Health Center
160 W. 100 St. (Amst - Col)
M - F 8:30-5; Th 8-6
R, downstairs, not WA.

St. Luke's Hospital
W. 113 St. (Amst- Morningside Dr.)
Daily 6:30-11pm
At the Visitors' Entrance go L, through doorway, (follow sign) L, through doorway.RRs are ahead on the L. At Emergency (open 24 hours) RRs are on the L.

Harlem District Health Center
158 E. 115 St. (Lex - 3 Aves.)
M - F 9-5
Take staircase on either side (or the elevator) to basement. Go L off the elevators. RRs aren't WA, but there's a sign to a WA toilet on the ground floor (back L - "Hypertension"). There are 5 steps at the entrance.

Boriken Health Center
2253 3rd Ave. (122-123)
M, Tu, Th, F 8:30-5; W 8:30-7:30
Enter R side of courtyard. Take elevator to 3rd floor. If you pass the reception desk on the R, then head straight ahead, you'll find a set of RRs across the waiting room. But water pressure (at least in the WR) is so bad, they're unflushable. Better ask the receptionist for another location.

North General Hospital
Madison Ave. (123-124)
Open 24 hours
RRs are right by the guard's station - ask guard to unlock.

Sydenham Hospital Neighborhood Family Care Center
215 W. 125 St. (ACP - FDB)
M - F 8-8; Sa 9-3
Take elevator to 2nd floor, go across the floor and down the corridor on the R. There's an unmarked door to the L of the desk. Press in the metal bar that's halfway up (watch your fingers!) and pull. WA. (While waiting for the elevator, notice the stickers on the newsstand. One says, "Black is Dutiful.")

Manhattanville Health Center
21 Old Broadway (126)
M - F 8:30-4:30
Go down the stairs at L; keep making lefts till you reach the RRs.

Harlem Hospital Center
506 Lenox Ave. (135-136)
Open 24 hours
(Lenox = Malcolm X Blvd.) The entrance on W. 136 St. is open when the main one is closed. "Male Toilet" and "Female Toilet" are just L of main entrance.

Central Harlem Health Center
2238 5th Ave. (136-137)
M - F 8:30-4:30

There's one "Patient Toilet" (WA) just inside the clinic entrance to your R. Undoubtedly there are others on the upper floors. There are 4 steps at the entrance.

 The Council's Center for Problems in Living
1727 Amsterdam Ave. (145)
M - F 8:30-8

Turn L just past the guard's desk. In the WR, the WA stall has a door; the other one doesn't.

❖ Auction Houses ❖

 Tepper Galleries
110 E. 25 St. (PAS - Lex)
Tu - Sa 9 or 10am - ?

Auctions about once a week with exhibition one or two days before that. On exhibition days, closes 5 or 7pm. Sometimes auctions begin 7pm on weekdays. RRs are on L near the back. The WR is not very elegant except for the gilt-framed mirror.

 Lubin Galleries
30 W. 26 St. (Bwy - 6 Ave.)
Every other Th 10-7; every other F 9-3; every other Sa?

Auctions are held every two weeks, on Sa, with viewing on Th & F. The RRs are on the L, halfway back.

 Christie's
502 Park Ave. (59)
M - F 10-5

Upstairs, RRs down hall to L of desk.

 Rena-Coa Multi-Service Center
1920 Amsterdam Ave. (155-156)
M - F 9:30 - 5:30

If door is locked, ring buzzer. Go downstairs, ask at the desk, head around R to RRs. WA.

Columbia-Presbyterian Medical Center
W. 168 St. (Bwy - Washington Ave.)
Daily noon - 8 (see description)

Past the guard's desk, about 1/3 of the way down the hall, is an overhead clock. Just past that are the RRs, the MR on L clearly labeled, the WR on R, just before the elevators, with the sign: "Sprinkler Control Valve for Gift Shop at Ceiling in Ladies Room." In case you're looking for an ATM, you'll pass one. Sign at entrance says "Visiting hours 12-8 except for ICUs," so you might get in anytime. If not, Emergency is on the same block, closer to Broadway.

 Christie's East
219 E. 67 St. (2-3 Aves)
Approx. M - Sa 9:30-5:30 or 10-5; Su 1-5

Auctions are scheduled several times a week, with viewing for several days beforehand. Hours vary. RRs are upstairs at L ("Gallery 2"); turn off when you reach the telephones. Fresh flowers are on the sink in the WR. Not WA.

 Sotheby's
1334 York Ave. (72)
M - Sa 10-5; Su 1-5

Down a few steps to L, RR sign will direct you down the corridor to your R.

 Phillips
406 E. 79 St. (1st - York Aves.)

Auctions are scheduled about once a month, with exhibitions 2 or 3 days beforehand. Weekday hours are 10-6 or 10-7, Sa hours may be 10-5, Su noon - 5. On auction days there may be 2 exhibition hours, 9-11 am, before auction starts. RRs are back R.

 William Doyle Galleries
175 E. 87 St. (Lex - 3 Ave.)
M 9-7:30; Tu 9-5; W 10-?; Sa 10-5; Su noon-5

Auctions seem to be weekly on Wednesdays, with exhibitions the previous Sa - Tu. Check bags at entrance; RRs are back L.

❖ Parks & Playgrounds ❖

 Battery Park/Castle Clinton
N. end of Battery Park
8:30 - 5 pm, year-round

RRs are within castle walls, and in stone building elsewhere in park: at north end, across from W.U.I. Plaza; at south end, next to playground.

 Carmine Street Pool
7th Ave. South (Clarkson St.)
M - F 5:30pm-10:30pm; Sa 12:30-5:30

Entrance on 7 Avenue South. WR on L, MR on R. WR has a sign: "Do not use sinks for garbage or disposal of Kotex," and stainless-steel sinks, mirrors and toilets - no seats. The WA stall was locked from the inside.

Washington Square Park
Washington Sq. S. (Thompson St.)
7am - 10 pm
Stone building on Wash. Sq. South (halfway along). No toilet seats - but they do have paper.

 Asser Levy Recreation Center
E. 23 St. (Asser Levy Pl.)
See below
Summer: M - F 7:15am -10:15pm; Winter: 7:30am - 9:30pm; Both: Sa & Su 10-5:15. Women's Locker Room is halfway down the corridor on R. Electric dryers are set high on the wall so they can be used for drying hair as well as hands. Separate door for "Physically Challenged/Disabled Women" was locked, but the men's counterpart was ajar. Couldn't spot the Men's Locker Room, but you'll have to ask the guard to let you in, in any case.

 E. 54 St. Recreation Center
348 E. 54 St. (1-2 Aves.)
M - F 3-10; Sa 10-5
Swimmers must sign in with ID; but the guard will let you in to use the RRs. WR: up the stairs on the R; not WA. MR: entrance on L just past the guard.

 John Jay Park
E. 77 St. & Cherokee Pl. (E. of York)
Across from the park entrance, near the river, is a dark-red brick building that's the entrance to the pool. The RRs are on either side of the entrance and are open 8-4.

 Riverside Park Playground
Riverside Drive (83)
2 Port-o-sans stand outside the stone building at the playground entrance. (RRs in the building itself are padlocked.)

 Riverside Park Playground & Wading Pool
Riverside Drive (97)
The stone building (surmounted by a stairway) has RRs.

Riverside Park Rotunda
Riverside Drive (79)
RRs are open only when there are shows at the Rotunda, according to members of the homeless (and bathroomless) community who live there.

 Hecksher Puppet House/Central Park
62 St., mid-park
Daily 8-5
Look for a brick building south of the ballfields, adjacent to 2 concrete adventure playgrounds, and just north of a conventional playground. The RRs aren't too bad.

 The Arsenal/Central Park
5th Ave. (65)
M - F 9-4:30
Take elevator to 3rd floor gallery. There's a MR to L of elevator. The WR is on the 2nd floor: turn L, go to end of hall. It's WA, but there are 14 steps at building entrance.

 Children's Zoo/Central Park
Near 5th Ave. (65-66)
Daily 10-5 (No admittance after 4:30)
"10¢ admission to Zoo and Restrooms." Girls and Boys are to L of entrance. In the WR, one of the sinks is at a child's height.

 Refreshment Stand/Central Park
67 St., mid-park
RRs are on the west side of the snack bar, which is decorated with trompe l'oeil trellises. The WR,when I visited, had no TP and was wet and filthy. Users have opted, from the looks of the wall around the flushing button, to operate it with their feet - a sensible move which I followed.

 Bethesda Fountain/Central Park
72 St., mid-park
From the fountain: go under the arches & halfway up the stairs. From the bandshell: go halfway down stairs. RRs are closed while bandshell area is under renovation. Closed in winter.

 Kerbs Memorial Building/Central Park
Conservatory Water near 5th Ave., (73)
The building is on the east side of the model boats pond. In the WR, one of the 2 stalls was unusably filthy.

 Loeb Boathouse/Central Park
75 St., mid-park
WA RRs, in nice condition, are on the east side of the boathouse.

 Delacorte Theater/Central Park
81 St., mid-park
RRs are in the building west of the theater. WR is on the northside, MR on the south side. WA but no grab bars. Pretty nice condition.

 Tennis House/Central Park
93 St., mid-park
Daily 7 am - sundown, April - November
A notice says the Tennis House will be closed over the winter (1991-92) for renovation. This implies that in future winters it'll be open.

 North Meadow Recreation Center/Central Park
97 St., mid-park
For MR, go under archway between buildings, to handball court. Turn R and R again. For WR: as soon as you pass pillars at entrance, turn L onto basketball court. Head for door at back L.

Lynn had been my theater-going buddy for a number of years, but we'd fallen out of touch. Whenever I phoned her she seemed happy to hear from me, but she never called me. This irritated me so much that I stopped calling.

Then one weekend after running an errand on the East Side, I walked through Central Park to the Upper West Side, where I intended to join the Central America Walkathon making its way down Broadway.

I got to Broadway early but I needed a bathroom. I phoned Lynn, who was home and happy to hear from me, and I stopped by to inspect the plumbing.

She had changed; so had I. We've been better friends ever since.

IFFY OPTIONS IN PARKS & PLAYGROUNDS
(not keyed to map)

Although there are "comfort stations" in almost all parks and playgrounds, many of them are open only sporadically due to staffing cutbacks. Additionally, unheated buildings close for the winter. Below are a selection of facilities, according to the Parks Department, that you may or may not find open.

East River Park	East River Drive (6)
Playground	Baxter & Bayard Sts.
St. Gaudens PG	2 Ave. (20-21)
St. Vartan's Park	1 Ave. (35-36)
McCaffrey PG	W. 43 St. (8-9 Aves.)
St. Catherine's Park	1 Ave. (67-68)
Playground	W. 70 St. (WEA - Amst)
Ancient Playground	Central Park (5 Ave. & 85 St.)
Playground	Amsterdam Ave. (94)
The Happy Warrior PG	Amsterdam Ave. (99)
Frederick Douglass PG	Amsterdam Ave. (101)
Playground	3 Ave. (108-109) MR, at least, open
Playground	RSD (124)
Howard Bennett PG	W. 135 & Lenox Terrace Pl.
Col. Charles Young PG	Malcolm X Blvd. (144)
Playground	W. 180 St. & Amsterdam
Bennett Park	Ft. Washington Ave. (185)
Payson PG	Payson & Dyckman Sts.
Playground	Riverside Drive (Bwy & Dyckman St.)

P19 **Conservatory Garden/Central Park**
5th Ave., (105)
Daily 8 am - dusk

There's a map of the grounds on a freestanding piece of wrought-iron fence to the L of the entrance. The WR is to the L, the MR to the R of the fountain and the vine-covered Wisteria Pergola behind it.

P20 **Asphalt Green/ George & Annette Murphy Center**
555 E. 90 St. (York - EEA)
M, W, Th 8am-10:45pm; Tu & F 8-9:45; Sa & Su 9-6:45

A "public/private" sports & arts facility. ID is required for entry to the building (a day pass costs $5), but no one asked me for mine. RRs are straight ahead, then L.

P21 **Pelham Fritz Recreation Center**
Mt. Morris Pk. W. & 122 St.
M - F 7am-8pm; Sa 8-6

Turn R. MR before, WR past drinking fountain. Not WA.

P22 **J. Rozier Hansborough Recreation Center**
35 W. 134 St. (5 Ave. - MX)
M - F 9am-10pm; Sa 10-6

The WR is on the L, the MR on the R. Enter the building via Lenox Terrace Place, leading from W. 135 St.

P23 **Maple Leaf Cafe/Ft. Tryon Park**
Margaret Corbin Drive
M - F 10-5; Sa & Su 10-6

RRs downstairs, cafe upstairs. Follow the signs north from Margaret Corbin Plaza - it's not far. For information on The Cloisters see listing E53.

P24 **Isham Park**
Seaman Ave. (Isham St.)

RRs are in a brick building between tennis courts and ballfield.

P25 **Carl Schurz Park**
East End Ave. (86)
Daily 9-3

RRs are in a red brick building between the 87th & 88th St. entrances. Posted hours are 9-3 daily; when I visited after 3, it was still open. (Other RR facilities in the park were closed.)

P26 **J. Hood Wright Park**
W. 174 St. & Ft. Washington Ave.
Daily 8-5

The MR is on the L side of the store building on the R. The WR is on the R side of the building on the L.

❖ BILLIARDS & OTHER INDOOR SPORTS

Q1 **Palm Billiards**
250 E. Houston St. (Aves A - B)
Daily 11am-3am

RRs are at back, to L of snack bar. They offer pool, video games, snacks, pingpong, backgammon, dominoes & air hockey. There's a sign on the bulletin board looking for a chess partner.

Q2 **Village Billiards**
75 Christopher St. (7AS- Bleecker)
Su - Th 11am-3am; F & Sa 11am-4am

Walk downstairs, turn R to the entrance, then L to the RRs. Pingpong, too.

Q3 **Corner Billards & Cafe**
85 4th Ave. (11)
See below

Non-summer hrs: Su - W 11am - 2am; Th - Sa 11am - 4am. Summer hrs: Su noon - 2 am; M - Th 11am - 2am; F 11am - 3 am. Le Country Gourmet Cafe at back, with an additional entrance on 11th St. RRs are at the back on the right.

Q4 **Le Q Billiards**
36 E. 12 St. (Bwy - Univ. Pl.)
Open 24 hours

Refreshment counter at front; RRs back L.

Q5 **Bowl-Mor Lanes**
110 University Pl. (12-13)
Su-W 10-1; Th 10 - 2; F & Sa 10 - 4

$3 per game per person, shoe rental 75¢ - no sneakers. Bar & Grill. There's a staffed elevator to take you to the 4th floor. RRs in the back, at the end of the lanes.

Q6 **Julian's Billiards**
138 E. 14 St. (3-4 Aves.)
Daily 10am-3am

RRs are L of the entrance - toilets only; the sink is outside. The 14th St. environs are sort of seedy, but the inside, while not glitzy, is well-maintained.

Pockets Billiards
7 W. 18 St. (5-6 Aves.)
Su - Th 11am-2am (if busy enough); F & Sa 11am - 3 or 4am.
Private RRs are toward back on L. This modern spot has a CD jukebox & a cooler stocked with sparkling water, non-alcoholic beer & non-alcoholic champagne. There's also a soda machine. Ladies play free 6-9pm every day.

Q8 Hackers, Hitters & Hoops
123 W. 18 St. (6-7 Aves.)
M - Th 11-11; F 11am - 1am; Sa 10am-1am; Su noon - 10pm
RRs are straight back past the Sport Court. They offer (take a deep breath!): minigolf, snack bar, batting cages, pingpong, air hockey, Orbotron, a driving video game, competition basketball, kids' playground, pool table, & a sport court where you can play basketball, volleyball, raquetball, paddle tennis, badminton & short court tennis.

Q9 The Billiard Club
220 W. 19 St. (7-8 Aves.)
M - Th 11pm-3am; F & Sa 11pm - 5am; Su 11pm - 1am
WR is back R; MR is halfway back on L. There's a nice snack bar with small pizzas, empanadas, etc. Some video games, too.

 West Side Rifle & Pistol Range
20 W. 20 St. (5-6 Aves.)
M - F 9am-11pm; Sa & Su 9-5
Downstairs - RRs along hallway to range. Targets are line drawings of a burly gunman aiming straight for you. "See Range Officer for Key" on RR doors. Do you want to ask for a key? I didn't.

 Society Billiards
10 E. 21 St. (5 Ave. - Bwy)
Su - Th 11am-midnight or later; F & Sa 11am-3 or 4am
This upscale place is downstairs. RRs are up a ramp to the R of the desk. Video screens & music; juice & soda at the desk.

Q12 Chelsea Billiards
54 W. 21 St. (5-6 Aves.)
24 hours
Pool, snooker & billiard tables. Large, lively (although dimly lit) room. RRs past the counter on the R about halfway back. Handicapped toilet & sink in WR. Stall doors a little small, like dressing room doors.

 Mammoth Club 26th
114 W. 26 St. (6-7 Aves.)
Open 24 hours
RRs are at back R on lst & 2nd floors. They've got pool, billiards, snooker, pingpong, golf putting, a driving range, a juke box & a half-dozen video games.

Q14 Midtown Billiards
371 W. 34 St. (9 Ave.)
Open 24 hours
This is an old-fashioned, un-spiffy 9-table place. Go upstairs; RRs are L, then R, past the desk.

 Midtown Golf Club
7 W. 45 St. (5-6 Aves.)
M - Th 11:30-9:30; F 11:30-2:30 + evening; Sa & Su 10-3
Take elevator to 2nd floor. The WR is just opposite. Not WA. MR: ?

Q16 West Side Billiard Club
601 W. 50 St. (11 Ave.)
Open 24 hours
(The entrance is on 11th Ave.) This stylish new club has 3 ornately-carved tables at the front, two with the overhead counters that you slide along the wire with the tip of your cue. There's a pingpong table, too. RRs are on R near front.

 Amsterdam Billiard Club
344 Amsterdam Ave. (76-77)
Su - Th 11am-3am; F & Sa 11am-5am
This trendy new spot has a cafe & a bunch of pale wooden benches - sort of a ski lodge atmosphere. Climb the stairs; RRs are halfway back on R.

 East Side Billiard Club
163 E. 86 St. (Lex - 3 Aves.)
M - Th noon-2am; F & Sa noon-3am; Su noon-1am)
This new place has music and videos. The RRs are R, just past the desk/snack bar. Not WA.

 BINGO
2465 Broadway (91-92)
M - Sa noon-2:30 or maybe 4, 7-10pm; Su 7-10pm
RRs are at back to L of the snack bar. Games start 12:30 & 7:30pm.

 Washington Heights Bingo Hall
St. Nicholas Ave. (181)
M - F 12:30-3, 7:45-10; Sa 12:30-3, 7:15-10; Su 7:15-10
Entrance is in the 181 St. subway station (#1 train). Admission is $1, but nobody seemed to mind my wandering around. RRs are at R front - not WA.

 Guys and Gals Billiard Parlor
500 W. 207 St. (Post - 10 Ave.)
Daily noon - midnight
Enter downstairs. Salsa music was playing and the folks seemed quite friendly, but I felt conspicuous (I was the only woman there) and I got shy. So I didn't ask where the RRs were; I assume they have some.

❖ RELIGIOUS BUILDINGS ❖

R1 Trinity Church
Broadway & Wall St.
M - F 7-6; Sa & Su 8-4
In the back, on the R. Free concerts Tuesday, 1pm.

R2 John St. United Methodist Church
44 John St. (Nassau-Dutch Sts.)
M - F 11:30-3
The hours given are those of the Wesley Chapel Museum. Facing the exit the WR is downstairs on the L; the MR, presumably, is on the R.

R3 St. Paul's
Vesey - Fulton, Bwy - Church
Daily 8-4; Su 7-3
Enter from Bwy (go through chapel) or Church St. graveyard. "The Rest Rooms are unavailable during services." Free noonday concerts Mon. & Thurs. (concert lasts 30-40 minutes). "Please see the Verger or the Security Guard for admittance".

R4 St. Luke in the Fields
487 Hudson St. (Christopher St.)
Garden open to public is at south end of block. Enter at the middle of the block and walk to the back. Across from the school, on your L is an open door with the sign, "Chapel Entrance." A few paces along the L-hand hallway is a private unisex RR. The chapel is open for services at 7:40am and 6:15pm and occasionally for other events.

R5 The General Theological Seminary
175 9th Ave. (20-21)
M - F noon-3; Sa 11-3; Su 2-4
The seminary oc cupies a full, fenced-in city block. Visitors are welcome at the outdoor garden, indoor exhibit, and the bookstore (open M - F 9:30-4:30, Sa 12:30-4:30). There's a playground on the west side of the grounds; as you walk the grounds you may encounter bicycle-riding children. For the WR, turn R past the desk, and R again at the first alcove. There's potpourri on the makeup table. MR: ?

R6 Episcopal Church Center
815 2nd Ave. (43-44)
Bookstore hrs: M - F 8:30-6
Bookstore on R - enter through lobby. RRs down corridor to R & back of guard's desk.

R7 Church Center for the UN
777 UN Plaza
M - F 9-5
(Entrance E. 44 St. west of 1st Ave.) RRs downstairs. Disabled 2nd floor.

R8 St. Clement's Church
423 W. 46 St. (9-10 Aves.)
M - F 10-6; Su 9am-11am
Ring bell at L doorway. The Vis-a-vis Gallery is upstairs; RRs are downstairs - entrance at the side of the stairs. At the foot of the stairs head R past the bookshelves, down the corridor. Not WA. (During the annual Ninth Ave. Food Festival, St. Clement's opens its RRs to the public.)

R9 St. Bartholomew's Church
Park Ave. (50-51)
RRs are left open only during services, but the guard will open them any time on request. Services Tu 12:10, W 1:10 & 6 pm, Th 12:10 & 5:15, Sa 5:15, Su 9 & 11 am. A row of beds in the outer lobby attests to their ministry with the homeless. The entrance to the thrift shop, open Tu-Th 11:30-3:30, is on 51 St.

R10 Central Synagogue Community House
121-25 E. 55 St. (Lex - Park)
M - F 9:30-4:30; Su 11-2
View the exhibit in the lobby or visit the Sisterhood Gift Shop (open till 4 pm). The security guard can direct you to the RR.

R11 NY Catholic Center
1011 1st Ave. (55-56)
M - F 9-5
Outside, before the revolving door, enter L. Before you enter the church ("To Parish Campaign") there's an unmarked door to the R. If it's locked, ask the security guard inside the lobby for access.

R12 Temple Emanu-el
1 E. 65 St. (5 Ave.)
Daily 10-5
Leave your bag under the guard's watchful eye. The sanctuary is to the L, the gift shop, with appealing toys & tchatchkes, is to the R. Just across from the gift shop is a glass door leading downstairs to the RRs.

R13 Mormon Visitors Center
2 Lincoln Sq. (at 65 & Col)
Daily 10am - 8pm
A volunteer will take you up to the Visitors Center on the 2nd floor, give you an introductory talk, sit with you through a 15-minute videotape, and answer your questions afterwards (total time about 40 min.). RRs are to the R in back of the reception desk. To skip the tour, you might just ask to pick up some literature from the Family History Center, which is also on the 2nd floor.

Minskoff Cultural Center
164 E. 68 St. (Lex - 3 Aves.)

Follow the L wall around the curve toward the back; the RRs are before the stairs. There's an exhibition, as well as the Judaica Center of NY (silversmiths) in the lobby. Open M - F 9-5 plus some evenings for basketball.

 Jan Hus Presbyterian Church
351 E. 74 St. (1-2 Aves.)
See below

Flea market: Sa 10-4 (Sept - June) Museum: M - F 5-7:30pm; Sa & Su 3-6pm. There's a unisex RR upstairs; turn R at the top of the stairs. On the ground floor, there are RRs at back L of the flea market space. The MR is straight ahead; for WR, turn L as soon as you pass through the first doorway.

 Oestreicher Community House/ Temple Shaaray Tefila
2nd Ave. (79)

RRs are to the R, The WR is very pink. "The Shop" (gift shop) is open M-Th noon -5, Su 10-1. The library on the mezzanine is open to non-members only on Tu from 10-3, when "the ladies" (?) are there.

 Congregation Rodeph Sholom
7 W. 83 St. (CPW - Col)
M - F 8am - ? (sometimes 10pm); Sa & Su ?

RRs are a half-flight downstairs. The WR has well-fitting doors, a couch and vanity table. The brass scrollwork doors at entrance are wonderful!

 Park Ave. Synagogue/Sherr Institute of Adult Jewish Studies
Madison Ave. (87)
M - Th 3-6; W 3:30-6:30; Su 9:30am-12:30pm

The hours given are those of the Rothschild Library. The guard will investigate your bags. Go straight ahead, then turn R, following signs for the coatroom. You'll hit the WR first, then the MR farther along around the bend.

 Lindenbaum Center
270 W. 89 St. (Bwy - WEA)
M - F 8am - sometimes 10pm

The WR, not WA, is down the hallway on R. The cafe doors on the stalls swing open, then close in the middle with more or less of a gap. MR: ? The Yonah Gallery is open Tu-Th 1-6.

Islamic Cultural Center of NY
1711 3rd Ave. (97)
Day and evening hours

Enter on E. 97 St (2-3 Aves.) and talk to one of the staff down the hall. Women will need to wear a head scarf; pants are OK. Remove shoes on 2nd floor to ascend to the mosque on 3rd floor. Visitors will be welcome at the back during services; women occupy a separate gallery. There's a "Charity" box at the entrance to the mosque. Spacious RRs are on the 2nd floor. WR: In the first section there's a marble foot-washing trough with marble-cube stools. Farther back are sinks and stalls, the stalls equipped with hand-held shower heads

for the required religious washing. The WA stall on the L was locked from the inside. The staff members were very gracious to me. Especially considering the ongoing level of Islamic-Western tension, I'd urge you to visit only if you're prepared to work at lessening that tension.

 Ansche Chesed Synagogue
251 W. 100 St. (Bwy - WEA)
M - Th 6:30am-10pm

RRs are downstairs: MR on L, WR on R. Not WA. (They run a shelter here every night except Saturday.)

 Cathedral Church of St. John the Divine
Amsterdam Ave. (112)
Daily 7-5

RRs are in back of the gift shop (open 9-5 daily), which is about two-thirds of the way into the cathedral, on the L. The facilities, a temporary installation, are of a rustic quality not out of place at the entrance to a state park. The gift shop is large, diversely-stocked and wonderful! There are also RRs downstairs: for WR take stairs on R, for MR stairs on L, both down long corridors.

 The Interchurch Center
W. 119-120 Sts., Claremont Ave.- RSD
M - F 8-6

On the Claremont side, take the escalator (or elevator) down. Go L, and L again past the soda machines to RRs. WA. The cafeteria, pleasant and cheap, is open 8-3. Bus your tray, with the crockery still on, down a slope on rollers. Wheel On the 1st floor on the Riverside Drive side, is the SERRV Gift shop, open 10-4. They've got a great selection of international crafts.

 Riverside Church
Riverside Drive - Claremont Ave, 120-122 Sts.
M - Sa 9am-10pm; Su 8:30am-5pm?

Enter at Claremont Ave. and what would be W. 121 St. Check out the exhibit in the Cloister Gallery. There are RR signs by the visitors' desk: MR is nearby, WR is down the hall. In the WR, the fronts and common wall of 2 stalls have been removed to make one WA stall containing 2 toilets with one grab bar on the far side of each. At the front there's a curtain rod but no curtain.

 Union Theological Seminary
Broadway (121)

Turn R at guard's desk. A little more than - halfway down the hall, just past the wall telephone, on L is an unmarked unisex WA RR next to another, not WA.

41

❖ Sightseeing ❖

S₁ NY Stock Exchange
20 Broad St. (Wall - Exchange Pl.)
M - F 9-4 (tickets run out about 1pm)

Self-guided tours begin every 45 minutes to an hour. Get a ticket from the ticket person standing outside 20 Broad St. Depending on demand and your timing, you may have to wait to line up. You'll definitely have to wait once you've lined up. Security is high: bag x-ray & walk-through metal detector. The gallery above the trading floor is now entirely glassed in, presumably in response to the disruption caused by Yippies throwing dollar bills in the 60's. The first batch of exhibits, plus gift shop, are arranged circularly. About 3/4 of the way around is an exit with adjacent MR. (WR is to L of the elevators - guard will let you in.) You can cut out now, or continue on to the other exhibits, the Experience Theatre (another wait) & the trading floor gallery (possibly another wait).

S₂ Hudson River Day Line - Pier 81
12th Ave. (41)
Closed at night

This pier is used only for special charters, but the guard will let you in on request.

S₃ Circle Line/ Hudson River Day Line - Pier 83
12th Ave. (42-43)
Open 24 hours

RRs on L, about 3 doors down.

S₄ United Nations
1st Avenue (45-46)
M - F 9-5; Sa, Su & Hols 9:15-5

Walk through the metal detectors, then take the elevator to the L of the information desk or the stairway to R. On the lower level, the WR is to the L, the MR is ahead and to the R.

S₅ Rockefeller Center
5-6 Aves., W. 49-51 Sts.
M - F 7am-7pm; Sa & Su 10-6.

If entering at 630 5 Ave. (50-51), go downstairs, bear L, go down marble stairs/ramp, and bear R alongside the American Festival Cafe. Leading off to the R is a newsstand and a Party Bazaar shop. Head R past them - the RRs are in that corridor. Wherever you enter the concourse, you can orient yourself by the Cafe and Party Bazaar.

S₆ Gray Line New York Tours
900 8th Ave. (53-54)
Daily 8-5 or 6

RRs on L of waiting room. Not WA.

S₇ NY Convention & Visitors Bureau/City Gallery
2 Columbus Circle (59)
M - F 10-5:30

The 2nd floor gallery is accessible by stairs or elevator. The RR is on the way to the gallery, and a flight of 5 steps separates it from the gallery level served by the elevator. What was formerly a MR (2 stalls, 1 urinal) has now been designated a "unisex restroom." The signs direct you to lock it from the inside. Since the policy on the ground floor is that there are no public RRs in the building, it might be politic to show some interest in the displays before asking the guard to unlock the RR.

❖ Theaters

❖ & Movies ❖

T₁ Angelika Film Center
Houston & Mercer Sts.
Su - Th approx. 10am-midnight; F & Sa approx. 10am-2am.

Private RRs to L of cafe. The cafe, with attractive food & drink, & paper (not foam!) hot cups, is open 10am-10pm.

T₂ Film Forum
209 W. Houston (Varick & 6 Ave.)
See below

The Film Forum is a rare treasure, not only for its distinctive film programs but for the accessibility of its RRs. No need to buy a ticket - bear L past the box office and you're there. It's hard to pin them down on their hours of operation, because it depends on the films. They open half an hour before the first film starts and close about 20 minutes after the last one ends. This works out to opening weekdays about 1:30 pm, weekends about 12:30 pm; and closing Su - Th about midnight, F and Sa often at 2 am (Midnight shows!).

T3 Anthology Film Archives
32 2nd Ave. (2 St.)
W & Th 6pm-11:30pm; F 6pm-12:30pm; Sa 1-11:15; Su 1-10:30

Hours vary with films scheduled; these are the outer reaches of the opening and closing times. You can pick up a two-month schedule anytime from the outdoor dispenser. RRs are down the hallway on the L. In the WR, the door has been removed from the end stall for wheelchair accessibility. Low toilet and no grab bars, though - and no door.

T4 The Living Theatre
272 E. 3 St. (Aves. C - D)

This cutting-edge anarchist theatre troupe with a long history in NY, Europe and South America has now found a home on the Lower East Side. The storefront entrance keeps erratic hours. M - F someone's there 1:30 - 5, possibly as late as 7:30. Restroom-seekers can't be accommodated during the performance.

T5 Public Theater
425 Lafayette St. (4 Ave. - Astor Pl.)
Daily 2 pm - 10pm

Spot the sign for the Anspacher Theatre at back L. Go through 2 doorways and follow the signs (to the L).

T6 Union Square Theatre
100 E. 17 St. (PAS - Irving Pl.)
M noon-6; Tu - Sa noon-8; Su noon-7
Down the stairs by the box office.

T7 Lincoln Center/Avery Fisher Hall
Columbus Ave. (64)
Daily 10am-10pm

(More precisely, the closing time is 1/2 hour after the end of the evening event.) WR is on the Columbus Ave. side & is accessible from the side entrance as well. The MR is on the west side, near the far plaza entrance. There are also Lincoln Center RRs down one level, on the way to the parking garage. One entrance is to the R of the box office entrance to the NY State Theatre. Walk down the stairs, turn L, turn R onto a promenade that includes an art gallery. These RRs may be open 24 hours.

T8 Symphony Space
2537 Broadway (94-95)

This former movie house, rescued from demolition, was reborn as a community cultural center, drawing its audience from all over the city. There's a free (or "pay what you will") evening event once a month or so; once or twice a year there's a "wall-to-wall" all-day event that's free, too. RRs are on the R past the stairway.

T9 Apollo Theatre
253 W. 125 St. (FDB-ACP)
M - Th 10-2

Hours given are Gary Byrd's live WLIB radio broadcast, to which the public is invited. RRs are downstairs to R of auditorium entrance (elevator also available). The gleaming WR is all black - toilets, stalls, marbled floor and sinks. Almost the only thing white is the TP. Audience members are free to come and go during broadcast.

❖ UNIVERSITIES & OTHER SCHOOLS ❖

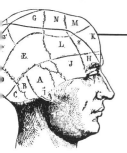

U1 Murry Bergtraum Business and Adult Education Center
411 Pearl St. (Madison St.)
M - Th 5pm-9pm

The entrance is on Madison St., near Pearl. RRs are straight down the hall on R, the MR halfway down, WR at the back. WR shows signs of seat-shpritzing and foot-flushing.

U2 Borough of Manhattan Community College (BMCC)
Chambers (Greenwich - West Sts.)
Bldg. open 24 hours, but reg. business hours are 10 - 6

Sign: "You must show your BMCC ID card or you may be delayed entering the college." I wasn't challenged. I assume this means that after business hours you will be stopped and will have to ask politely to use the RRs (unless there's a performance in the Triplex Theatre).

U3 New York Law School
53 Worth St. (Church - W. Bwy)
M - F 8am-11pm; Sa & Su 8am-10pm

RRs are on L at the back of "B" Building (53 Worth) but also accessible through "A" (#47) and "C" (#57).

U4 NYU/Waverly Building
Waverly Pl. (WSE - Greene St.)

On the 2nd floor by the elevators there's a MR, a WR, and a "Handicapped." These may be the closest RRs to the Grey Art Gallery at 33 Washington Pl., with hours Tu, Th & F 11-6:30, W 11-8:30 & Sa 11-5.

U5 Hebrew Union College/Jewish Institute of Religion
E. 4 St. (Bwy - Mercer St.)
M - Th 9-5 or 8; F 9-4

RRs are in back of the receptionist. WA. Sometimes NYU classes are held here in the evening.

NYU/Loeb Student Center
566 LaGuardia Pl. (4)
M – W 8-10:30; Th 8-midnight; F 8-7
RRs are downstairs. The MR is at the foot of the stairs; turn R for the WR. Via elevator, the MR is across the hall, the WR to your L. Usually on weekends the building is open only to students with ID, but sometimes there are public events.

 Cooper Union Great Hall
Cooper Square (7)
Daily 8am-midnight
The entrance is at the south end of Cooper Square, adjacent to E. 7 St. Go downstairs, to the end of the hall (there's an exhibit along the way), L, then R. WA.

 The New School
66 W. 12 St. (5-6 Aves.)
Maybe M – F 7am-10pm; weekends till 5pm (sometimes closed Su)
On the ground floor, to the R of the auditorium entrance, there's a MR "1/2 flight down." MR & WR also on 3rd floor - take elevator.

 Benjamin N. Cardozo School of Law - Yeshiva University
55 5th Ave. (12-13)
Su – Th 9-5
Sign in at the guard's desk to visit The Gallery, a wall of art exhibits on R side. At the back, turn L to the RRs.

 Parsons School of Design
5th Ave. (12- 13)
Daily 8am-10pm
MR is in the R corner of the back exhibition room. WR is in the space past that, also on the R. Around the corner at 2 W. 13 St (5-6 Aves) is another exhibition space, open M-Sa 9-6, W 9-9. WR is on a white, iron-railed balcony on the R; MR is at the foot of the stairs.

 Mabel Dean Bacon H.S.
127 E. 22 St. (Lex)
Tu &Th 6pm-9pm
Go through the doorway at back R, and down the corridor to private "Teachers-Women" and "Teachers-Men."

 Baruch College Gallery
135 E. 22 St. (Lex - 3 Ave.)
M – F noon-5; Th noon-7
The WR is at the end of the bank of elevators, on the R. MR: ?

School of Visual Arts
209 E. 23 St. (2-3 Aves.)
M – F 8am-10pm
As you might expect, there's an art exhibit in the lobby. RRs are at the back.

 SUNY State College of Optometry
100 E. 24 St. (Lex-PAS)
M – F 8am-10pm; Sa 8-5
Look for a big overhead sign, "RESTROOMS" on the R. WA.

 Fashion Institute of Technology/ Shirley Goodman Resource Center
W. 27 St. (7 Ave. SW corner)
Tu – F noon-8; Sa 10-5
Make 2 rights to the RRs. WA. ID is required in the other buildings on 27 St. (7-8) but you might find a guard who'll let you sign in as a visitor.

Norman Thomas H.S.
E. 33 St. (Park - Lex)
A sign on the door announced a 5:30pm opening. I followed students up the escalator, up & up, to the 7th floor. "Girls" was directly to the R. Around the corner R of the entrance to the down escalators, was the "Boys." NYU courses are given here evenings - I'd guess M - F. Other floors are probably OK too.

CUNY Graduate Center
33 W. 42 St. (5-6 Aves.)
M – F 8am-10:30pm; Sa 9-5
In the walkway to 43 St, go down one flight, walk straight to the back, turn R, then L. Not WA. The Dining Commons on the 18th floor is open M - F 8-8; take elevators on the L. WR: go R, take first L (before you reach the tinted-glass entrance to the bar). MR: as above, but then make another L, past the drinking fountain.

Wilfred Beauty Academy/American Business Institute
1657 Broadway (51-52)
See hours below.
ABI: M - F 8am-9:30pm; Sa 9-3. Wilfred: M - Th 9:20-4:50, 6:20-9pm; F 9:20-4:50; Sa 8:45-4:45. The MR is at the entrance to ABI, on the 2nd floor. The WR is at the entrance to Wilfred, on the 3rd floor.

Art Students League
215 W. 57 St. (7 Ave. - Bwy)
WR: Go R to the inside office, down to the end, R and through the door, and downstairs. MR: ?

John Jay College of Criminal Justice
445 W. 59 St. (9-10 Aves.)
M – F 7am-11pm; Sa & Su 9-7
There's an exhibit on the lobby walls at back. For RRs, go straight back at L through the green doors; turn L. 899 10 Ave (58-59) is a modern building constructed behind and below an elegant 1903 facade. Daily hours are 9-6 or 7. Go down escalator; first R.

 Alliance Francaise
22 E. 60 St. (5 - Mad Aves.)
Library hrs: M – Th 10-8; F 10-4
RRs on lower level - the stairway's on the r

Hunter College Student Center
Lexington Ave. (68)
Daily 8am-10pm

Take escalator to 2nd floor, turn R (elevator, too). You might also want to check out the bookstore on the main floor, and the snack bar on 2.

 Marymount Manhattan College
221 E. 71 St. (2-3 Aves.)

The Gallery is open till 10pm. For the WR turn R, continue down to end - it's on the R. MR:?

 CUNY
535 E. 80 St. (York- EEA.)
Open 24 hours

Ask the guard: the WR is on the L, MR on the R. They're WA, although there are 3 steps at the entrance.

 NY Academy of Medicine
2 E. 103 St. (5 Ave.)
M - F 8-5

MR is on ground floor, WR on 2nd. The Cafeteria on the 5th floor is open 8am - 2pm ("All welcome!!!") "[Most] programs... are open without fee to members of the medical & allied professions... No advance registration is required." There's a library, too.

 Bank St. College
610 W. 112 St. (Bwy - RSD)
M - F 9am-evening

The WR is back L. WA. MR: ? The cafeteria downstairs is open to the public M - Th till 6 and F till 3.

 Columbia University/ St Paul's Chapel
Amsterdam Ave. & W. 117 St.
M - F 11-8

(There's a Wheelchair Accessibility Map of the campus posted justed inside the main gate (B'way & 116) on the L.) The Chapel is the red brick bldg. with a polygonal tower east of Low Library. In addition to the above hours, when the chapel is open for "meditation, quiet study & prayer," the Postcrypt Coffeehouse downstairs (free admission) is open F & Sa from 9pm. The Postcrypt Art Gallery is open Tu - F 2-6 and Sa 9pm - 12:30am. Services of various denominations on Tu & W run past 8pm, on Sa run 11am-1pm, and on Su are scheduled for 7am, 11:30, 5, 7, 8 & 9pm. On Th there are often free noontime organ recitals. RRs are downstairs to R of entrance.

 Columbia University/Buell Hall
College Walk, W. 116 St. (Bwy - Amst)

This building, in back of Low Library, is home to an Architecture Exhibition, the Maison Francaise and various offices. From the lobby, open the door to the South Gallery to find 2 private unisex RRs on L. WA but no grab bars. RRs are available even when offices are closed.

 Columbia University/Kent Hall
College Walk, W. 116 St. (Bwy - Amst)
M - Th 9-7; F 9-5; Sa 12-7

This building, housing the East Asian Institute, is south of St. Paul's Chapel, east of Low Library. RRs are on the 5th floor (2 flights up from entry level), between the X and Y staircases. The WR, not WA, features nostalgia-evoking Nik-o-lok "Pull Down" shelves to stash purses on.

 Columbia University/Earl Hall
Broadway & W. 117 St.
M - F 9-5

This is the domed building northwest of Low Library. The back of the building is accessible from Broadway & 117th via an iron gate. The Commons Cafe is open 9-2:30 (salad bar: 11:30-2:15). The building is sometimes open evenings and weekends, including Su 10-2 for Quaker Meeting for Worship (you're welcome to join them for shared meditation). There's wheelchair access to the building on the south side; RRs, not WA, are downstairs.

 Barnard College
Broadway (117)
M - F 9:30 am - 8:30pm ?

A sign reports "Restrooms are on the 2nd & 3rd floors of Barnard Hall," closer to the north end of the building.

 City College of NY
Convent Ave. (138)

Most buildings need ID, but asking politely brought results. The first building I tried is open 7am-10pm. Freeest access is to the North Academic Complex, a new building complex on the lower level west of Convent Ave. at about 137 St. WR is on R side of escalator, MR on L.

 Yeshiva University Museum & Library
2520 Amsterdam Ave. (184-185).
Tu - Th 10:30-5; Su noon-6

There's a $3 admission to the museum, but you should be able to use the RRs without paying. Turn L; go past the elevators. The WR is downstairs, MR upstairs. Not WA. Across the floor is the Gift Shop. Even when closed, the gift items are left on display in glass cases. Guards, if asked, may admit you to other buildings, with a wider range of hours, for RR visits.

 Stuyvesant Youth and Adult Center
345 E. 15 St. (1-2 Aves)
M - Th 6pm-9pm; Sa 9am-noon

The adult education classes here operate on a more limited schedule than the public school system: the Fall Semester, for instance, starts Oct. 19. For RRs, go up the L stairway (or take elevator), turn R, then L down to the end of the hall.

❖ STORES ❖

V₁ Sym's
42 Trinity Pl. (Rector - Edgar Sts.)
Tu - W 8-6:30; Th, F 8-8; Sa 10 - 6:30; Su 11:30-5:30

"Closed Monday - Except Certain Holidays". RRs 2nd floor, north end. They're straight ahead as you descend the escalator from the 3rd floor.

V₂ Century 21
22 Cortlandt St. (Bwy - Church)
M - F 7:45 - 7; Sa 10-6
RRs downstairs in "Personnel." No one under the age of 21 permitted without parent or legal guardian.

V₃ Forman's of Orchard St.
59 John St. (William St.)
M - Th 7:45 - 6:30; F 7:45-4; Su noon-5
Ask at desk for key to WR.

V₄ Pearl Paint
308 Canal St. (Bwy - Mercer St.)
M - W, F, Sa 9-5:30; Th 9-7; Su 10-5:30
No need to buy, but you should be able to find something you want in this discount department store of art supplies, craft supplies & stationery items. Get key at front from security guard. Unisex RR is at back L.

V₅ Barney's
7th Ave. (16-17)
M - Th 10-9; F 10-8; Sa 10-7
M & W on lower level toward the back of the store. Easiest access is by the W. 17th St. entrance (the first awning down from 7th Ave.).

V₆ ABC Carpet & Home
888 Broadway (19)
M & Th 10-8; Tu, W, F 10-7; Sa 10-6; Su 11-9
The elevator is on the R side of the building. RRs, not WA, are on floors 2 & 4; go R off the elevator. The WR has modern fixtures with a period flavor: an overhead tank with a pull chain.

V₇ Lerner's
W. 34 St. (5-6 Aves.)
M - F 9-8; Sa 10-6; Su noon-5
MR & WR to the L of the grand staircase at the back. Look for the EXIT sign - go through an unmarked door to the R. A gleaming private facility which, when I visited, was out of paper.

V₈ Macy's
6 - 7 Aves., 34-35 Sts.
M, Th, F 10-8:30; Tu, W, Sa 10-7; Su 11-6
MR - 4 & 7; WR - Cellar, 2, 6 & 7.

V₉ Lord & Taylor
5th Ave. (38-39)
M & Th 10-8:30; Tu, W, F, Sa 10-6:30; Su noon-6
WR - 4th & 5th floors, MR- 10th.

V₁₀ Lane Bryant
5th Ave. (39-40)
M - Th 10-8; Tu, W, F, Sa 10-7; Su noon-5
"Take elevator [at back of store] to 2nd floor & make a right. Someone will open the [unmarked] door for you if it's locked." It wasn't. 2 doors marked "Restroom."

V₁₁ Brooks Brothers
346 Madison Ave. (44)
M - F 8:30 -6; Th 8:30-7; Sa 9-6
WR - 3rd floor, MR - 5th.

V₁₂ Saks & Company
611-621 5th Ave. (49-50)
M - W, F, Sa 10-6:30; Th 10-8; Su noon-6
WR - 4th floor, MR - 6th. (Restaurant on 8 - probably one there too, inside.)

V₁₃ Henri Bendel
5th Ave. (55-56)
M - W, F, Sa 10-6:30; Th 10-8; Su noon-6
WR - L, 3, 4; MR - L.

V₁₄ Galeries Lafayette
E. 57 St. (5 - Mad Aves.)
M - W, F, Sa 10-6:30; Th 10-8; Su noon-5
WR on 5th & 6th floors; MR on 6th floor.

V₁₅ Tiffany's
5th Ave. (57)
M - Sa 10-5:30
RRs are on the Mezzanine. Elevators and stairs are at back of store. Walkers, beware: it's 3 flights up. When you get there, turn L.

V₁₆ Bergdorf Goodman
5th Ave. (57-58)
Daily 10-6; Th 10-8; Su closed. W & E side of avenue, same hours.
The women's store, on the west side of 5th Ave., has W & M RRs on the 7th floor. The men's store, on the east side of 5th, has a WR on 2 and a MR on 3.

V₁₇ FAO Schwarz
5th Ave. (58-59)
M - W, F, Sa 10-6; Th 10-8; Su 12-6
Entrance also on Mad. Ave. From 5th Ave. entrance, go up escalator, L, then R.

V18 Alexander's
3 - Lex Av~~~~
~~CLOSED~~
RRs ~~noon-5~~
~~oor.~~

V19 Bloomingdale's
Lex. - 3 Aves., 59-60 Sts.
Th 10-9; M, Tu, W, F, Sa 10-6:50; Su 11-6
WR - 4th & 7th floors; MR - LL, 5th & 7th floors

V20 The Limited Express
691 Madison Ave. (62)
M - F 10-8; Sa 10-7; Su noon-5
Go through the doorway to L of the elevators. Turn L past the security guard and head down the hall filled with cartons and racks of clothing. Jog L and you'll find a WA unisex RR.

V21 Ralph Lauren
867 Madison Ave. (71-72)
M - Sa 10-6; Th 10-8
Take elevator to lower level; turn R. The WR stalls are entirely private; there are outsize soft paper hand towels. (If you wander through the store, be warned that the air on the 3rd floor - ladies wear - is heavily perfumed.

V22 Bargain World
8 W. 125 St. (5 Ave - MX)
M - Sa 9-6:30
Unisex RR on 3 floor. Take stairway to 2nd floor. Cross the floor to the R, take another stairway to 3rd floor.

❖ WAR (USO) ❖

W1 USO Metropolitan NY
151 W. 46 St. (Bwy - 6 Ave.)
M - Sa 10am-9pm; Su 11am-7pm
Take the elevator to the Gen. MacArthur Memorial Center on the 3rd floor. They offer a pool table, TV, VCR, video games, tourist info, free tickets, hotel reservations, snacks and, presumably, RRs to members of the military.

❖ TRANSPORTATION CENTERS ❖

X1 Staten Island Ferry Terminal
Broadway (Water St.)
Open 24 hours
When reconstructed after fire, 50¢ admission will again be collected. This will give access to terminal RRs as well as to the ferry. Using the ferry RRs will probably commit you to a one-hour round trip (not necessarily a bad thing!). Until reconstruction passengers enter on ground level behind terminal and pay upon exit on Staten Island.

X2 PATH/World Trade Center
Church - West Sts., Liberty - Vesey Sts.
Daily 5am-2am
The RRs at the entrance to the PATH trains (a commuter subway to New Jersey) are the only public ones in the World Trade Center. The WR has a sign, "Closed for repairs Wednesday 9:30 - 11:30am until further notice."

X3 Penn Station
7-8 Aves., W. 31-33 Sts.
Open 24 hours
Entrances are on 7th Ave at 32nd St., and 8th Ave. at 31st & 33rd Sts. The Amtrak and NJ Transit terminal is one flight down - RRs are in the NW corner of the bldg. One more level down is the LIRR terminal - the RRs are on the east side of the building, to the L of the ticket windows.

X4 Port Authority
40-42nd Sts., 8-9 Aves.
Daily 6am-1am
Limited admittance 1am - 6am for ticket holders only to the downstairs bus bays. RRs on lower level, 1st & 2nd floors.

X5 Grand Central Station
42 St. (Vanderbilt & Lex)
Daily 5:30am-1:30am
Entrances on all 3 sides. WRs - between 42nd St. & the MOMA shop. You'll find it most easily by using the easternmost entrance on 42nd St. MRs - corridor leading to subway alongside ramp leading down from corner of 42nd St & Vanderbilt Ave. (west end of terminal).

X6 Lexington IRT Subway Station
E. 86 St. (Lex)
What a surprise! There are men's & women's RRs on both the uptown & downtown local platforms. The platform worker will unlock on request.

I was traveling overnight from Dharmsala to New Delhi on the video bus with Frances, my newly-made English friend. Every few hours the bus would pull into a station and we'd stagger out into the cold night air to look for a toilet. At one stop I wandered around, then finally asked a young man. He pointed me to the right door, and was waiting when I emerged.

"Did you relieve yourself?" he asked, beaming.

SPECIAL NEEDS/CONCERNS

My thanks to Disabled in Action for raising my consciousness about wheelchair accessibility. Another friend told me of his need for a private, lockable space: he's a diabetic, and doesn't like to freak people out when giving himself an injection.

Some people need more privacy than that provided by conventional toilet stalls, where people can peer in through the spaces on both sides of the doors. The comments about stall-door coverage stem from my experiences in the much-more-private restrooms in Europe, and from the overheard complaints of foreign visitors here (as well as the complaints of us natives!).

 Freda, my elegant Viennese friend whom I met years ago at a peace conference and who has since become a member of the Austrian Parliament, was in town. After walking through Central Park on a crisp fall day, we ended up on Madison Avenue.

Freda needed to pee. I wanted to be a good hostess. What could I suggest? We walked anxiously for several blocks, looking for a likely restaurant. (Now, post-research, I could easily suggest a hotel.) Finally we sighted a cozy-looking French bistro with people clustered at the front, waiting for tables.

"Aha!" I cried. "Go in there. They'll assume you were lined up with the rest." And so she was able to empty her bladder unchallenged.

But what must she think of us?

X7 **125th Street Railroad Station**
E. 125 St. (Park)
There are no RRs in the station, but, offers a
helpful ticket seller, "If you have to go bad--
the gas station," as he points across Park
Avenue.

X8 **GW Bridge Port Authority Bus
Terminal**
Broadway & 178 St.
Daily 5am-1am
Standing by the ticket windows, the WR is
directly to the L of the newsstand; the MR
farther L, past the Haircutters.

❖ Y's, Settlement Houses & Community Centers ❖

Y1 **Educational Alliance**
197 E. Broadway (Jefferson St.)
M - Th 9-9; F 9-6; Su noon - 6
The entrance to the New Gallery is on the L.
RR are downstairs to the R of reception desk.

Y2 **Henry St. Settlement Arts Center**
Grand St. (Bialystoker Pl. - Pitt St.)
Daily 10 - 6
RRs downstairs.

Y3 **Grand St. Settlement**
80 Pitt St. (Rivington St.)
M - F 8:30 - 6, some evenings
(The building entrance is actually a bit east of
Pitt St.) Turn L at entrance; RRs are on the L.

Y4 **Lillian Wald Settlement**
12 Ave. D (3)
M - F 9-5
The entrance is east of Ave. D - a sign on a
building says "Manhattan St." Turn L for RRs.
WA.

Y5 **Sixth Street Community Center**
638 E. 6 St. (Aves. B - C)
M - F 9-5
There's a large private unisex RR down the
corridor on L. Not WA.

Y6 **Jacob Riis Community Center**
80 Ave. D (6-7)
M - Th 8:30am-9pm; F 8:30-5
RRs are halfway back on R. Not WA. In the
WR, the toilets have been fitted with smaller
seats, for smaller bottoms.

Y7 **Greenwich House Pottery**
16 Jones St. (Bleecker - 4)
Tu - Sa 1-5
Ring the bell. The Gallery is on the 2nd floor,
to the R at the top of the stairs. There's a
private unisex RR, not WA, across the hall, on
the L just inside the doorway.

Y8 **All-Craft Center**
23 St. Marks Pl. (2-3 Aves.)
Open 24 hours
RRs are towards the back on the R, the WR
closer to the front, MR closer to the back. The
WR wasn't in great shape when I visited -
more what you'd expect from a park facility.

Y10 **Hudson Guild**
441 W. 26 St. (9-10 Aves.)
*M - F 9am-11pm; Sa 8am - possibly 1am; Su it
depends*
Stop at desk, please. Then turn R; RRs are
along the corridor, on the L, MR almost
immediately, WR just a little farther. The Art
Gallery, at R front, is open M - F 11-7.

Y11 **Goddard-Riverside Community Center**
593 Columbus Ave. (88)
M - F 8:30-5:30
RRs are on the R, past the first R.

Y12 **92nd St. Y**
1395 Lexington Ave. (92)
M - Th 10-9; F 10-4; Sa 6-9pm; Su noon-8
(Closed weekends in summer.) Go up ramp,
get clearance from guard, head R down
corridor, get clearance from another guard,
turn L.

Y13 **Union Settlement**
237 E. 104 St. (2-3 Aves.)
M - F 9-5
Enter the unlabeled doorway on the L side of
courtyard, RRs are on the R side of the room,
across from the reception desk.

Y14 **Grosvenor Neighorhood House**
176 W. 105 St. (Amst)
M - F 9:30am - 9:30 or 10pm
The RRs in this unlabeled building are on the L
side of the corridor just past the guard's desk.
Not WA. The WR features one of the last
working dispensers of interfolded rectangular
TP in the city.

Y15 LaGuardia Memorial House/Corsi House
307 W. 116 St. (Manhattan Ave. - FDB)
M - F 9-5

At the entrance, photo exhibits feature LaGuardia, Corsi, and "East Harlem Heritage." Take the short stairway or elevator up to the continuation of the exhibition. Turn R, then take the first L down the corridor to the RRs. WR: one stall is wheelchair-size, but no grab bars.

Y16 Joseph P. Kennedy, Jr. Memorial Community Center
34 W. 134 St. (5 Ave. - MX)
M - F 8am-9pm; Sa & Su it depends

RRs are downstairs at the Auditorium entrance. Enter the building via Lenox Terrace Place, leading from W. 135 St.

Y17 James L. Varick Community Center
151 W. 136 St. (ACP - MX)
Daily 7am - 10pm

RRs are down the hall on the R. They're WA, as you might have guessed from the ramp at entrance.

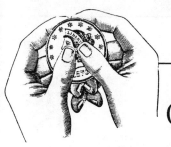

❖ FINANCIAL AID ❖
(WELFARE, SOCIAL SECURITY, ETC.

$1 NYS Unemployment Insurance
50 Park Place (W. Bwy - Church)
M - F 8:30-5

Ramp up to office, but toilets (on L) not WA. Keys are in wire basket on guard's desk.

$2 US Social Security Office
231 Grand St. (Bowery - Elizabeth Sts.)
M - F 8:30-4

Take elevator to 3rd floor. There are 2 unisex WA toilets to R. No TP when I visited.

$3 US Social Security Office
85 Delancey St. (Allen - Orchard Sts.)
9 - 4:30

Take elevator to 3rd floor. RRs R off elevator. Single unit M & W. WA

$4 NYC HRA Income Maintenance Center
12 W. 14 St. (5-6 Aves.)
M - F 8:30 - 5

RRs on L wall.

$5 NYC HRA Food Stamps
109 E. 16 St. (Irving Pl - Union Sq. E.)
M - F 8-5

Turn L; RRs are at the end of the the corridor. Not WA.

$6 US Social Security Office
38 E. 29 St. (Park - Mad)
M - F 9-4:30

Take the elevator to the 5th floor of this posh office building. The guard will escort you and will unlock the door to the unisex (non WA) toilet.

$7 NYC HRA Amsterdam IMC
260 W. 30 St. (8 Ave.)
M - F 8-5

Go L past the windows, and L again.

$8 NYC HRA IMC
225 E. 34 St. (2-3 Aves.)
M - F 8:30-5

From the main entrance: go straight down the hall, turn R. From the R entrance: down hall, turn L.

$9 NYC HRA Medicaid Office
340 W. 34 St. (8-9 Aves.)
M - F 8-4:30

Take escalator to the 2nd floor, go a little L, then R. RRs are down the corridor on the R. (Or use the elevators at 330 W. 34 St. to the 2nd floor.) There was no TP, and the door was off one of the two WR stalls when I visited.

$10 US Social Security Office
237 W. 48 St. (Bwy - 8th Ave.)
M - F 9-4:30

Take elevator to 5th floor; turn R to find private WA RRs. Guard will unlock on request.

$11 US Social Security Office
133 E. 58 St. (Lex - Park)
M - F 9 - 4:30

Posh office building. Take elevator to 12th floor. Go L, then R across the floor to the private MR & WR. WA.

$12 NYC HRA IMC
309 E. 94 St. (1-2 Aves.)
M - F 9-5

Take elevator to 3rd floor; turn R. The MR is before, the WR past, the drinking fountain. Not WA.

$13 Social Security Office
306 E. 111 St. (1-2 Aves.)
M - F 9-4:30

Ask guard. Go through gate at his R & head toward the green "Rest Rooms" sign halfway back. There are single-unit M & WRs, but with no lock on the door. They're not WA, but there's a ramp at entrance.

NYC HRA IMC/Food Stamps
132-140 W. 125 St. (ACP - MX)
M - F 8:30-5

Go up stairs or take elevator to 2nd floor. Go through the L entrance (Undercare Interview Area) and take the 2nd R ("BEGIN Program"). RRs are on the L.

 NYC HRA IMC
165 E. 126 St. (3 Ave.)
M - F 8:30-5

(There are also entrances on E. 127 St. & 3rd Ave.) There's a RR down the hall on L with a "Closed" sign. Take elevator to 3rd floor, go through the doorway, turn R and R again. (There are signs mentioning WA toilets on other, unspecified floors.)

 NYC HRA Medicaid
520 W. 135 St. (Amst - Bwy)
M - F 9-5

The RRs are on the L near the entrance. This WR was pretty dirty, with no TP, when I visited.

 NYC HRA Food Stamp Program
1387 St. Nicholas Ave. (179-180)
M - F 8:30-5

Take elevator or stairs up to office (there's one step up at the entrance). Turn L past the clerks' windows, then R. WA.

 Social Security Office
4292 Broadway (182 St.)
M - F 8-4:30

L, down the ramp, L again.

 NYC HRA IMC
4660 Broadway (Dongan Pl.)
M - F 8:30-5

RRs are across the floor, a little to the L.

EVEN MORE PLACES

I'm not telling you all of the places I've discovered. Many of them are not very public, and access would be closed off for security reasons if traffic became noticeably heavier. I won't tell you about the office of a small publication that has an unlocked Ladies' Room just outside the door. I won't name the damaged-clothing store that offers you the toilet as a try-on room. And it won't help you to know the name of my dentist in the Williamsburg Bank Building, where I once stopped by to use the restroom on my way to the Brooklyn Academy of Music.

But whatever your interest, from growing bromeliads to collecting model trains - politics, religion, personal growth - there's probably an organization in New York City that would welcome your inquiries. And the staff probably would let you use the restroom while you're there.

To protect these places from hordes of needy restroom-seekers, I haven't keyed them to the map. But if you're interested, look them up in the phone book, stop by and check them out.

War Resisters League - pacifist group working against war and for social justice (sells books, buttons, bumperstickers)

C. G. Jung Center - institute & bookstore

New York Theosophical Society - institute & bookstore

Henry George School of Social Science - classes in George's land-based economics theory

Workmen's Circle - Jewish classes, cultural events & bookstore

Integral Yoga Institute - classes, bookstore & health food store

Lesbian & Gay Community Service Center - cultural events, exhibits and lots of literature about what's going on in the community.

WHAT DOES THE FUTURE HOLD?

Change.
   Some places will close; others will open. Hotels and hospital extensions are being built as you read this.
   There is a trend to limit restroom access. Many branch libraries are now off-limits to restroom-seekers. A number of hotels have installed punch-in combination locks at the entrances to their restrooms. I hope this trend is not accelerated by the publication of this guide. I hope the portable toilets which the city is now trying out will solve our problems. I hope this book will raise everyone's consciousness so that restroom-seekers will be welcome everywhere.
   But I could be wrong.
   If you know of restrooms I haven't mentioned, I hope you'll tell me; write to the address on the back cover. If demand exists I'd like to do a second edition with updated listings and complete information about wheelchair accessibility.

CHILDREN AND ELDERS

My friend Nathan, who has two small children, says that finding restrooms for them is not difficult - people are usually friendly and accommodating. He imagines that a parent with child in tow could approach a public-school guard for access to any school.
   And if you're a Senior Citizen (or can pass for one) there are Senior Centers all over the city.

I heard this story fourth-hand; I will tell it as it was told to me.
   A woman needed a restroom, but it was late and not many places were open. She spied a funeral parlor and went in. A functionary greeted her at the door.
   "Yes, may I help you?"
   Too embarrassed to ask for the Ladies' Room, she scanned the board with the list of funerals scheduled.
   "I'm here for the Johnson funeral," she offered.
   Under the usher's watchful eye, she entered her name and address into the Visitors' Book. Then she found the Ladies' Room, used it and promptly left.
   Several weeks later she received a check for $500. As the accompanying letter explained, Mr. Johnson had provided in his will that everyone who attended his funeral was to be given $500.